VAULT GUIDE TO LABOR & EMPLOYMENT LAW CAREERS

© 2003 Vault Inc.

The media's watching Vault!
Here's a sampling of our coverage.

"Unflinching, fly-on-the-wall reports... No one gets past company propaganda to the nitty-gritty inside dope better than these guys."
— **Knight-Ridder newspapers**

"Best way to scope out potential employers...Vault has sharp insight into corporate culture and hiring practices."
— **Yahoo! Internet Life**

"Vault has become a de facto Internet outsourcer of the corporate grapevine."
— **Fortune**

"For those hoping to climb the ladder of success, [Vault's] insights are priceless."
— **Money.com**

"Another killer app for the Internet."
— **New York Times**

"If only the company profiles on the top sites would list the 'real' information... Sites such as Vault do this, featuring insights and commentary from employees and industry analysts."
— **The Washington Post**

"A rich repository of information about the world of work."
— **Houston Chronicle**

VAULT

> the most trusted name in career information™

VAULT GUIDE TO LABOR & EMPLOYMENT LAW CAREERS

TIMOTHY GRUBB, VERA DJORDJEVICH AND THE STAFF OF VAULT

Library of Congress Cataloging-in-Publication Data

Grubb, Timothy.
  Vault guide to labor & employment law careers / Timothy Grubb, Vera Djordjevich and the staff of Vault.
      p. cm. -- (Vault career library)
   ISBN 1-58131-183-4
   1. Labor laws and legislation--Vocational guidance--United States. I.
Title: Vault guide to labor and employment law careers. II. Title: Guide to labor & employment law careers. III. Title: Labor & employment law careers. IV. Djordjevich, Vera. V. Vault (Firm) VI. Title. VII. Series.
   KF299.L3G78 2003
   344.7301'023--dc21

                                                              2003006733

Printed in the United States of America

ACKNOWLEDGEMENTS

Timothy Grubb's acknowledgements

Countless lawyers on both the management and plaintiffs' side of the labor and employment practice provided invaluable insight for this project. I thank you for sharing your experiences with law students who will become the next generation of labor & employment lawyers. I also want to thank Brent Giddens, Mia Montpas, and Glenn Briggs for fueling my interest in the labor and employment practice and for providing guidance on so many aspects of my legal career.

Vault also would like to acknowledge the support of:

Matt Doull, Ahmad Al-Khaled, Lee Black, Eric Ober, Hollinger Ventures, Tekbanc, New York City Investment Fund, Globix, Hoover's, Glenn Fischer, Mark Hernandez, Ravi Mhatre, Carter Weiss, Ken Cron, Ed Somekh, Isidore Mayrock, Zahi Khouri, Sana Sabbagh, and other Vault investors, as well as our family and friends.

If you have what it takes to be #1, we want to make you number 376*

Of all the firms surveyed in the *2003 Vault's Guide to the Top 100 Law Firms*, only two had everything it took to be named as the top labor and employment law firm: We were one of them. We're Littler Mendelson, the nation's largest, and most respected, employment law firm. And if you think you have what it takes to join the approximately 375 attorneys in 29 offices that compose the firm, we'd like you to become number 376.

And while numbers aren't everything, there are a few of them we thought you might be interested in:

9,600, as in the number of associates who made up the survey that ranked us in the top ten in terms of diversity for women, minorities, and alternative lifestyles.

500, which refers to the *Fortune 500* and the significant number of listed companies, and leading business like them, who choose Littler Mendelson to litigate, mediate and negotiate labor and employment matters on their behalf.

And lastly, **one,** as in YOU, and top graduates like you, who have the intelligence, dedication and creativity to keep us where we've been for the last 60 years, at the forefront of labor and employment law.

To find out more about becoming ONE of the nation's top 376 or so employment attorneys, contact Karen Herz at 415.433.1940, or visit us online at www.littler.com.

LITTLER MENDELSON®

A PROFESSIONAL CORPORATION

THE NATIONAL EMPLOYMENT & LABOR LAW FIRM®

650 California Street, 20th Floor, San Francisco, CA 94108.2693
Tel: 415.433.1940 Fax: 415.399.8490

Table of Contents

GETTING HIRED 55

APPENDIX

People

Experience

Development

Opportunity

www.blackwellsanders.com

Introduction

It's no secret – the practice of labor and employment law has exploded recently. Over the past few decades, the relatively stable practice of labor relations has become one of the busiest areas in the legal profession. The number and scope of anti-discrimination statutes continue to expand, as employment discrimination cases flood the dockets of state and federal courts across the country. In addition to traditional labor-management disputes and employment rights claims, lawyers face a dizzying number of legal issues related to the workplace, including employee benefits, wage and hour compliance, trade secret and unfair competition disputes.

Unlike other practices, fluctuations in the economy determine the nature of a labor/employment lawyer's work more than they affect the volume of his or her workload. In a strong economy, employment lawyers work with client companies to expand their employment policies and fine tune their human resource practices. They also advise corporate attorneys on the employment-related aspects of mergers and acquisitions and other transactions. During an economic downturn, layoff reviews take center stage, and employment litigation heats up as workers who have suffered real or perceived wrongs are more likely to bring claims against former employers in a tough employment environment. In short, a career in labor and employment practice can be a safe bet no matter what the economic climate is. Given the uncertainty of today's economy, such stability can be enormously appealing.

Perhaps the buzz around this legal hotspot has inspired you to get in on the action. This book will guide you through the various careers available in labor and employment law. "The Scoop" provides a general overview of the substance of labor and employment law, including the federal statutory frameworks and government agencies commissioned to enforce employment and labor laws. The first chapter in this section explores the "employment" half of labor and employment law, including employment litigation and employer counseling, often considered the mainstay of the modern employment practice. The second part discusses "traditional labor" law, the oldest branch of this growing practice area, which refers to matters involving organized labor unions and the companies whose workers are unionized.

In "On the Job," we will take a more detailed look at what labor and employment attorneys actually do and sample a "Day in the Life" of five different lawyers. Finally, "Getting Hired" outlines the various places to practice labor and/or employment law and suggests strategies for landing that perfect job. While this guide cannot give you specific directions on how to become a labor or employment lawyer, it can serve as a roadmap, highlighting the kinds of work attorneys encounter, places where you might practice and how to get started.

THE SCOOP

Employment Law

CHAPTER 2

Overview of Modern Employment Practice

Labor and employment practice as we know it was born during the turbulent 1960s. While the United States was invading Vietnam, back home battles were being fought over social and political issues, including women's rights, free speech and the growing anti-war movement. In 1964, in the midst of these developments, Congress passed Title VII of the Civil Rights Act, which would become the foundation of the equal employment opportunity movement. Title VII prohibits an employer from discriminating against an employee or applicant with regard to hiring, firing, compensation, terms, conditions or privileges of employment based on a "protected characteristic." Protected characteristics under Title VII include race, color, sex, national origin and religion. Federal statutes modeled after Title VII brought additional characteristics under the scope of federal protection. For example, in 1967, the Age Discrimination in Employment Act (ADEA) added age to the list of protected characteristics, and in 1990 the Americans with Disabilities Act (ADA) added physical and mental disabilities.

Following the federal government's lead, nearly every state adopted fair employment practice statutes modeled after Title VII. In fact, some state laws now go beyond Title VII and provide more sweeping protection for employees. California's Fair Employment and Housing Act (FEHA) incorporates additional protected characteristics (such as medical condition and marital status) and is generally more protective of employee rights than the federal statutes. Title VII also established the Equal Employment Opportunity Commission to enforce the provisions of these federal anti-discrimination laws.

Litigation, counseling and transactional work: the basics of employment practice

For many attorneys, employment practice is litigation-focused, and these lawyers spend much of their time litigating cases under Title VII, related federal laws or their state equivalents. At employment boutiques, many small firms and some large law firms, associates might spend up to 80 percent of their time on litigation-related matters. If you shy away from litigation-oriented clinical courses and hate civil procedure and moot court, employment practice may not be for you. On the other hand, if the thought of litigation gets you excited, there might be no better place to practice than in the employment arena. Employment discrimination cases are some of the most exciting cases around. Hardly a week goes by without a discrimination claim hitting the news or popping up in an episode of *The Practice* or re-runs of *Ally McBeal*. Other employment litigation can involve wage and hour violations, wrongful termination, employee benefits, trade secrets and countless other conflicts arising out of the workplace.

Not all employment attorneys are heavy-duty litigators; at some larger firms, employment litigation may be handled by the general litigation department while employment lawyers focus on counseling and transactional work or corporate support. Other employment attorneys on the management side spend a significant amount of time on transactional matters, working with colleagues in other departments like corporate, tax and finance, to advise on the employment- or benefits-related aspects of proposed mergers and acquisitions or to assist in due diligence.

In addition to litigation and transactional work, employment attorneys counsel clients on matters ranging from the benefits for an individual employee to broader issues like layoffs or restructuring. The extent of counseling a particular lawyer engages in will depend on the nature and structure of her firm. Some employment attorneys report that non-litigation counseling can take up to 40 percent of their time; for others, counseling forms a relatively small part of their practice.

The amount of time individual attorneys devote to each of these areas – litigation, transactional work and counseling – varies from firm to firm, as well as from associate to associate. Litigation may be the bread and butter for small firms and employment boutiques, but for some large firms with in-house corporate departments, corporate support might play a more substantial role.

Cases with personality

Employment litigation passes the "cocktail party test" with flying colors. While their colleagues discuss derivative suits, reverse triangle mergers and obscure patent claims, employment litigators talk about the deep, dark secrets of the workplace next door – the "sexy" cases that often make their way into the headlines and cost big companies serious money. Employment litigators love the human interest of their practice. They also appreciate the intriguing scenarios that form the basis of many employment cases. In fact, one of the first things many employment litigators say they enjoy about their practice is that it is all about people. Employment cases are never about Bank X suing Corporation Z over a multimillion-dollar contract gone bad. They are about real people and real emotion.

Many employment lawyers enjoy digging into the personality issues at the heart of their cases. Getting a feel for the personal side of a case may entail parsing e-mails, interoffice memos, performance evaluations, personnel files or psychiatric reports. Every new case involves a unique and highly personal story – one of actual or perceived indignities suffered, a job lost under troubling circumstances or accusations of egregious conduct on the job. The ever-changing factual scenarios keep employment lawyers keenly interested in their work even after decades of practice. The hours you work as a litigator may tire you out, but you will almost never be bored.

Nevertheless, there is a less glamorous aspect to close involvement with the personal aspects of a case. Lawyers may be reviewing personnel records with an eye toward mass layoffs or terminating an individual employee. As one management-side associate remarks, "It can be very depressing to sit at a company for days on end reviewing the personnel records and work histories of lists of employees who will be out of work just as soon as you finish." On the other hand, if the employment lawyer sometimes feels like an executioner, the same attorney may take solace in his role as "guardian of the employment laws designed to promote fairness in the workplace" by helping temper emotional reactions and suggesting strategies to improve a particular employee's performance or handle a "bad apple."

The dynamic nature of employment law

Plaintiffs who bring successful employment discrimination suits are often awarded economic damages for lost wages, as well as damages for emotional distress. Moreover, employers can be slapped with punitive damages hefty enough to cause any CFO to lose sleep. Verdicts in employment cases are nearly always made, for better or worse, by juries. The inherent unpredictability of jury verdicts heightens the element of risk for both sides.

Adding another level to the intrinsic volatility of employment practice are the laws themselves, which are always fluctuating. Employment lawyers must keep abreast of these changes, as old laws are amended, new laws are passed and judges interpret the subtleties of statutes. In view of the frequency with which employment-related cases reach the Supreme Court, keeping up with decisions that could alter the face of landmark statutes is both essential and exciting. The dynamic and evolving nature of employment law ensures that attorneys will remain intellectually challenged throughout their careers.

More pros and cons of employment practice

Many employment attorneys specialize in one substantive area of the law, in contrast to their counterparts in other areas of commercial litigation, for example, where practitioners must learn a new body of law for each case they litigate. Sarah Bouchard, a senior associate in the labor and employment department at Morgan, Lewis & Bockius, believes that this aspect of the practice allows attorneys on the management side to improve their litigation skills while gathering expertise that enhances their counseling on employment matters. Similarly, mastery of one set of substantive laws enables employment lawyers on the plaintiffs' side to focus less energy on legal research and devote more time to other aspects of the litigation process, like preparing briefs and developing a trial strategy.

On the flip side, practitioners say specialization "has certain drawbacks." As one lawyer with both boutique and big-firm experience observes, specializing in the relatively narrow field of employment law can make it hard to transfer between law firms, since attorneys will only be hired if there is an opening in that department, and employment departments are typically not very large. Another attorney highlights the broader issue of partnership prospects; for those associates not looking – or not likely – to make partner, it's worth bearing in mind that in-house employment law positions are "few and far between," so that an experienced employment lawyer might have less chance of going in-house than, say, a corporate attorney.

Similarly, while employment litigation can be exciting and dynamic, it doesn't come without headaches, and practitioners must deal with much of the unpleasantness that attorneys in other litigation-centered practices encounter daily. Court deadlines are demanding and often dominate lawyers' schedules and personal lives. Trials can be taxing and exhausting. Dealings with opposing counsel are often difficult and highly confrontational. In short, hours can be as long for labor and employment lawyers as for lawyers in other practices.

Cases Encountered by Employment Lawyers

Employment discrimination

The writers for even the trashiest daytime soap opera couldn't dream up the kind of mischief that occurs daily in the American workplace. Employment lawyers handle cases involving allegations of overt racism, repeated sexual harassment, and discrimination based on age, religion or disability. Litigating these cases and, on the management side, advising corporate clients how to contain current claims and avoid future claims make up the bulk of the employment litigation practice. Discrimination cases are litigated either as single- or multi-plaintiff lawsuits involving a single employee or a small group of employees, or as class action suits involving a larger number of plaintiffs who all share the same protected characteristic and suffered the same type of damage. For the sake of efficiency, the non-class action cases that involve single or multiple plaintiffs will simply be referred to as "single-plaintiff" cases.

Under Title VII, there are two basic theories under which a discrimination claim can be brought: "disparate treatment" and "disparate impact." In a disparate treatment case, the plaintiff must prove that the employer intentionally discriminated against him based on a protected characteristic such as race, sex or age. In a disparate impact case, there is no need to prove intentional discrimination; the employer can be liable even for seemingly neutral employment practices that disproportionately impact a protected class of employees. Disparate treatment cases are almost always brought as single-plaintiff actions, while disparate impact cases are commonly litigated as class action suits.

Disparate treatment and the single-plaintiff case

In the landmark 1973 case of McDonnell Douglas Corp. v. Green, 411 U.S. 792 (1973), the Supreme Court laid down a three-step framework that provides the basic template to which nearly all disparate treatment cases conform. Under McDonnell, the plaintiff must first establish a prima facie case of discrimination. In the example of a hiring case, the plaintiff would do this by proving the following four elements: (1) that she is a member of a protected class; (2) that she applied for and was qualified for a job for which the employer was seeking applicants; (3) that, despite her qualifications, she was rejected or suffered some other "adverse employment action"; and (4) that, after her rejection, the position remained open and the employer continued to seek applicants from people with the same qualifications as the plaintiff. In the second step, the burden shifts to the defendant (usually the employer), who must prove that the adverse employment action was taken for legitimate, non-discriminatory reasons. Then the burden falls back on the plaintiff, who must prove that intentional discrimination was the real motive behind the decision at issue.

This framework was applied in the recent Supreme Court case of Reeves v. Sanderson Plumbing Products, Inc., 530 U.S. 133 (2000). The plaintiff in Reeves was a 57-year-old manager who was terminated after an audit of his department allegedly revealed that he was not accurately tracking the attendance of hours worked by employees he supervised. The plaintiff brought suit under the ADEA, claiming that he was the victim of age discrimination. The plaintiff made out a prima facie case by establishing (1) that he was in a protected class under the ADEA because he was at least 40 years old; (2) that he was qualified for his position because he had been performing competently in that position for years; (3) that he suffered an adverse employment action because he was terminated; and (4) that the employer hired three people in their 30s to fill his position after he was terminated.

The employer then met its burden on rebuttal simply by alleging that the plaintiff was terminated because of his failure to maintain accurate records. (At this stage the accuracy of the employer's suggested reason is not challenged.) The final burden then shifted back to the plaintiff, who produced substantial evidence that the real motive of his termination was age discrimination. The plaintiff showed that he had continually maintained accurate records during his employment and that any discrepancies were attributable to the company's automated timecard machine rather than the result of his error. The plaintiff also produced specific evidence of age bias by introducing comments made by the supervisor responsible for his termination, including remarks that the plaintiff "was so old [he] must have come over on the Mayflower" and that he "was too damn old to do [his] job." The Supreme Court held that, by undermining the accuracy of the employer's explanation and introducing specific evidence of age bias, the plaintiff produced enough evidence to support the trial jury's finding that the employer unlawfully discriminated against the plaintiff based on his age.

Fact-intensive cases

Because the McDonnell Douglas framework applies regardless of which protected characteristic the plaintiff claims was the basis for an adverse employment action, employment litigators try gender discrimination cases in essentially the same way they try cases based on age or race discrimination. Therefore, it can be said that single-plaintiff cases are light on legal analysis but very fact-intensive. Those lawyers who loathe the thought of dealing with the overwhelming amount of documents involved in most commercial litigation cases will appreciate the relatively small volume of documents involved in most single-plaintiff employment cases. According to David Wimmer, an employment litigator at the labor and employment boutique of Swerdlow Florence Sanchez Swerdlow and Wimmer, the documents in a single-plaintiff discrimination case are both "manageable and masterable."

Single-plaintiff cases can be emotional undertakings for both employer and employee, and employment lawyers often assume the role of a trusted counselor. Because such cases are usually staffed quite leanly, with only one or two lawyers on each side, employment litigation can provide junior associates with substantial client contact and early exposure to substantive work, such as deposition taking and motion drafting. Employment litigators might have a handful of these single-plaintiff actions active at any one time. An individual case can last anywhere from one to two years, depending on the pace of the court where the case is filed. In state courts operating with a "fast-track" schedule, these cases might go to trial in under a year in some situations. Although many employment cases reach the trial (and even the lengthy appellate) stage, most discrimination cases, whether a single-plaintiff or class action, settle before trial or are dealt with by a dispositive motion, such as a motion for summary judgment.

Disparate impact and class action litigation

Class action discrimination cases are likely to be brought under a "disparate impact" theory and begin with the important (and often hotly contested) step of class certification. In class actions brought under such a theory, there exists a three-stage burden-shifting framework similar in structure to the McDonnell Douglas approach. In the first stage, the plaintiff has the initial burden of showing that the employer uses a particular employment practice (such as an aptitude test, educational requirement or other job selection device) which causes a disparate impact on a particular class who share a protected characteristic. This burden is met through detailed statistical analysis of the employer's workforce and/or the employment workforce in the geographic area most appropriate for comparison. (This group is called the "relevant labor market.")

Once the plaintiff (often the Equal Employment Opportunity Commission, as the federal agency responsible for enforcing Title VII) establishes a prima facie case of discrimination through statistics as well as evidence of specific acts of discrimination, the burden shifts to the employer. At this stage, the employer can specifically rebut the plaintiff's showing or it can prove that the challenged practice is closely related to or necessary for the job in question and is consistent with "business necessity."

For example, in the Supreme Court case of Dothard v. Rawlinson, 433 U.S. 321 (1977), the employer's use of minimum height and weight requirements for prison guards was challenged as having a disparate impact on the number of women that qualified for the position. A disparate impact was easily shown because these requirements would exclude about 22 to 33 percent of women in the national workforce (as compared to excluding only about 1 percent of males). In rebuttal, the employer attempted to show that the height and weight requirements were closely related to the physical strength necessary for adequate performance as a prison guard. The argument was ultimately unpersuasive, and the Supreme Court held that the employer should simply devise a test directly measuring strength rather than rely on height and weight requirements as decisive indicators.

If an employer succeeds in establishing that a practice which causes a disparate impact is job-related and consistent with business necessity, the burden then shifts back to the plaintiff. In this final stage, the plaintiff must show that there are less discriminatory but equally effective alternative practices available to the employer.

Lots of documents

Class action discrimination cases are often based on statistics and involve a massive amount of complicated documents and data. Class action lawyers frequently rely on the assistance of outside experts in statistical analysis, such as accountants and mathematicians. Employment litigators are not usually involved in more than one or two class actions at a time simply because of the volume of intense work these cases generate. Class action suits are also staffed with significantly more attorneys than single-plaintiff cases and the substantive work is often performed by senior attorneys (which is not surprising, given the potential liabilities in such suits).

Sexual harassment

Sexual harassment is a form of gender discrimination under Title VII. These cases, most often single-plaintiff actions, present unique challenges for employment litigators and are not subject to the McDonnell Douglas framework that governs most discrimination cases. Under EEOC guidelines interpreting Title VII, sexual harassment falls into one of two categories. Harassment is "quid pro quo" when a supervisor explicitly conditions a term of employment on the employee's submission to a request for sexual favors. This is the classic scenario in which a supervisor claims he will either fire a subordinate if she does not, or offer benefits if she does, engage in sexual conduct with him. The more common species of sexual harassment case is the "hostile work environment," which, according to the EEOC guidelines, occurs when "unwelcome sexual advances, requests for sexual favors, and other verbal or physical conduct of a sexual nature . . . [have] the purpose or effect of unreasonably interfering with an individual's work performance or creating an intimidating, hostile, or offensive working environment." Hostile work environment claims can arise in a variety of circumstances ranging from sexually explicit e-mails to unsolicited fondling by a manager or co-worker.

In Harris v. Forklift Systems, Inc., 510 U.S. 17 (1993), the plaintiff was a manager at an equipment rental company. The president of the company repeatedly made sexist remarks to the plaintiff in front of customers and other employees (e.g., "You're just a woman, what do you know?" and "We need a man as the rental manager."). The president also repeatedly asked the plaintiff and other female employees to reach in and retrieve coins from the front pocket of his pants. After the plaintiff asked him to stop, the president continued with sexual innuendoes and ploys like dropping objects on the floor in front of the plaintiff and asking her to pick them up so that he could look down her blouse. The Supreme Court held that this conduct was actionable as sexual harassment so long as the plaintiff's working environment would reasonably be perceived, and was actually perceived by the plaintiff, as hostile or abusive. The standard laid out in Harris remains in force today.

Under the Harris framework, a defendant can avoid liability under Title VII by asserting as an affirmative defense (1) that he exercised reasonable care to prevent and promptly correct sexually harassing behavior, and (2) that the plaintiff employee unreasonably failed to take advantage of any preventive or corrective opportunities provided or to otherwise avoid the harm caused by the abusive behavior. In order to succeed, the defense must show that the employer had comprehensive anti-harassment policies in place, such as reporting procedures and written manuals, that were vigorously enforced.

(Enforcement can take the form of, for instance, immediately recording incidents of harassment or confronting the alleged harassers with actual or threatened discipline.) The defense also needs to show that the plaintiff failed to report the harassing behavior or otherwise take advantage of the procedures in place.

Employment lawyers often spend much of their time counseling companies on sexual harassment issues. Employment lawyers may help human resource executives create company-wide policies that deal with sexual harassment and formulate appropriate complaint procedures. In addition, employment litigators on the defense side often counsel their clients on how to respond to the conduct of certain employees that may leave the company vulnerable to a harassment claim.

Wrongful termination

If an employee claims that his employment was terminated because of his membership in a protected class, that claim falls into the category of discrimination cases discussed above. But employment lawyers often encounter other varieties of wrongful termination disputes. Examples of wrongful termination claims that are distinct from discrimination claims include the breach of an implied employment contract not to terminate without just cause and "whistleblower" cases in which an employee is fired for reporting the employer's illegal conduct. These wrongful termination claims may be brought on their own or coupled with discrimination or sexual harassment claims. Unlike discrimination cases, wrongful termination cases are usually brought under state laws and judicial doctrines rather than federal laws.

The California Supreme Court case, Guz v. Bechtel National, Inc., 24 Cal. 4th 317 (2000), provides an example of a wrongful termination claim. The plaintiff John Guz was let go when the employer decided to shut down the plaintiff's department and transfer the work to another department within the company. Guz sued his former employer for age discrimination, breach of an implied contract to be terminated only for good cause and breach of the implied covenant of good faith and fair dealing. On his implied contract claim, Guz argued that the abrupt departmental closing violated an implied employment contract providing that he would be employed so long as he was performing satisfactorily and would be discharged only for "good cause." Guz cited his long tenure at the company as well as raises, promotions and good performance reviews as evidence of the implied contract assuring him continued employment. He also claimed that the employer's written personnel policies supported his claim because they provided for certain discipline programs and layoff protections (such as possible reassignment) that would be followed prior to termination. He argued that these procedures were not followed in his case.

In response, the employer claimed that Guz's employment was "at will" and could be terminated at any time. The defense asserted that the employer had established a personnel policy which explicitly stated its employees were not guaranteed continued employment and they could resign or be terminated at any time. The outcome in Guz was a complicated one, involving remand to a lower court on various issues, but the facts of the case provide a good picture of what a wrongful termination case often looks like.

Wage and hour litigation

The Fair Labor Standards Act is the federal statute that determines wage standards, such as minimum wage rates and overtime wages. The FLSA also lays out exemptions from the minimum wage and overtime provisions for certain high-level employees. Wage and hour litigation is an area of employment law that has been heating up recently, especially in places like California where state law is more exacting than the federal standards provided in the FLSA. The hottest area in the wage and hour arena is exemption class actions, in which large classes of employees claim they were denied overtime wages because they were illegally misclassified as exempt employees.

In a recent case in California, Bell v. Farmers Insurance Exchange, 87 Cal. App. 4th 805 (2001), a class of 2,400 insurance claims adjusters argued that they were misclassified as exempt "administrative employees" when they should have been paid hourly and overtime wages. The trial judge found that the claims adjusters were indeed wrongly classified and therefore entitled to back pay for all of the unpaid overtime hours they worked during the class period; the appellate court later agreed. A jury awarded the class a whopping $90.01 million in back pay, the largest verdict ever awarded in an overtime wages case.

These large wage and hour class actions, like discrimination class actions, are document-intensive and involve detailed statistical analysis. Moreover, the battle is usually won or lost at the class certification stage. A high-profile case such as Bell will often spur employers to call in their lawyers to make sure that they are in compliance with all applicable wage and hour provisions. Employment lawyers' duties at this stage might include wage and hour audits in which they analyze the job details of certain exempt employees to ensure that their position actually falls under a federal or state exemption.

Unfair competition, trade secrets and related litigation

Employment attorneys are exposed to the "softer side" of intellectual property law when they help their clients protect valuable and confidential business information from misappropriation by employees. This area of employment practice entails more counseling and preventive advice than actual litigation. Employment lawyers often draft and counsel employers on the enforceability of "non-compete" clauses or covenants, under which employees agree not to work for a competing company within a certain period of time after leaving the original employer. Employment lawyers also draft and enforce agreements in which employees acknowledge that they will be working with "trade secrets" and agree not to disclose any information regarding those trade secrets to any party without the employer's consent.

Actual litigation in this area usually involves a situation in which an employee leaves the original employer, moves to a new company in a related field and allegedly discloses to his new employer confidential information acquired at the original employer, such as a "formula, pattern, compilation, program, device, method, technique, or process" (Cal. Civ. Code §3426.1(d)'s definition of a "trade secret"). In this kind of trade-secret litigation, management-side lawyers often assume the role of plaintiff's counsel because their employer clients are suing the individual ex-employee and/or his new employer.

Employee benefits

Employee benefits law is a specialized area of employment practice in which counseling plays a large role. An attorney might advise an employer-client how to structure the company's health benefits in general, or outline the kind of medical benefits to which a specific employee is entitled. In 1993, the federal government enacted the sweeping Family and Medical Leave Act, which entitles employees to up to 12 weeks of leave in a 12 month period for family medical concerns, such as the birth of a child or a serious illness suffered by the employee or her child, spouse or parent. The Pregnancy Discrimination Act of 1978, an amendment to Title VII, dictates that pregnant employees must be treated in the same manner as other job applicants or employees with similar abilities or limitations. Employment benefits lawyers might spend much of their time counseling employers on how to comply with these federal laws and similar state provisions. In addition, employment litigators tackle discrimination claims that arise from alleged denial or unequal provision of employment benefits.

Some employment lawyers counsel or represent clients regarding the Employment Retirement Income Security Act of 1974. ERISA is a federal statute regulating the employee benefit plans of private employers. Employment lawyers might also be involved with other employee benefits issues, ranging from disputes as to whether an employee is entitled to unemployment benefits to negotiating compensation packages for high-level executives at major corporations.

Client counseling

Employment lawyers often spend much of their day fielding phone calls from clients to discuss issues that range from mundane human resources problems to complex business planning decisions. Some examples of the many workplace-related issues about which employment lawyers counsel their corporate clients include:

- Guidance with respect to a specific employee's hiring, discipline or termination (e.g., "Can I fire the guy with the nose ring?")

- Rights regarding leave for jury or witness duty

- Privacy issues stemming from Internet or phone use

- The restructuring of a business entity or reduction in a client's workforce

- Employee benefits issues such as severance packages, pension benefits and early retirement options

- Assistance with layoff decision-making

- Possible discrimination claims resulting from layoffs or firings

- Drafting employment, severance or non-compete agreements

Lawyers also draft and update employment manuals, analyze their clients' hiring practices and train employees on issues like sexual harassment. According to Connie Michaels, a labor and employment partner at San Francisco-based Littler Mendelson, this type of work is "more common when the economy is good." During rough economic times, such matters are often placed on the back burner while employers deal with more pressing issues like layoffs and restructuring.

It should be said that client counseling generally comes only after immense experience. Employment lawyers who are new to the field spend their time becoming proficient in the law and do not spend much time, if any, dispensing advice to clients. One senior-level associate at a large firm, whose practice includes only about 20 percent counseling, suggests that most client counseling is relegated to partners.

Transactional work

One facet of employment law which, according to an experienced attorney, is "increasingly part of a sophisticated practice" is transactional work, or corporate support. Employment lawyers at medium and large law firms might spend a fair amount of time working with the firm's corporate or finance attorneys, advising them on the employment-related aspects of corporate transactions like mergers and acquisitions. For example, a firm representing the buyer on a transaction might have an employment attorney review the employment-related representations in a proposed agreement to ensure that the buyer is not assuming unwanted liabilities, such as pending litigation or extensive severance obligations. Lawyers also assist in compiling and reviewing "due diligence," paperwork compiled during the investigation of a company targeted for merger or investment. Specifically, attorneys might determine whether the company's employment practices meet legal requirements or whether a company with a unionized workforce has labor problems. Such corporate-related work will probably constitute a larger portion of an employment attorney's practice when the economy is strong and M&A activity is high.

Statutory Framework

The EEOC: Uncle Sam's enforcer

The Equal Employment Opportunity Commission is the federal agency charged with enforcing the federal employment laws. These laws include Title VII, the ADEA, Titles I and V of the ADA, the Equal Pay Act of 1963, the Rehabilitation Act of 1973 (prohibiting discrimination against federal employees with disabilities) and the Civil Rights Act of 1991 (providing monetary damages in cases of intentional discrimination). The EEOC is headquartered in Washington, D.C., but has 50 field offices in cities across the country. The EEOC administers equal employment opportunity regulation, interprets federal employment laws and coordinates with state and local Fair Employment Practices Agencies that are like smaller EEOC's in their respective regions. For example, in California the Department of Fair Employment and Housing executes some of the same functions of the EEOC with respect to California's employment laws, and in New York the state Division of Human Rights enforces New York's Human Rights Law. These related state agencies nearly always follow the lead of the EEOC. While the EEOC is charged with many duties, its most visible function is litigating cases or resolving claims on behalf of employees who may have been the victims of discrimination.

The litigation process

The employment litigation process begins with the EEOC. Before a plaintiff employee can bring a suit in federal court, he or she must go through the EEOC. The process starts when the employee files a charge with the agency alleging that he or she was discriminated against. The EEOC investigates the charge to determine if there is "reasonable cause" to believe that the plaintiff was actually the victim of discrimination. The EEOC receives around 80,000 of these charges in a year. If the EEOC finds reasonable cause and the charge is not dropped, the agency attempts to mediate, so that the parties can reach a voluntary settlement (called the "conciliation process"). If a voluntary settlement cannot be reached, the EEOC has the right to file a suit on behalf of the plaintiff. Most charges, however, result in the EEOC issuing a "Right to Sue" notice to the plaintiff.

A Right to Sue notice simply means that for any number of reasons the EEOC has decided not to take any action and the plaintiff can now file suit in federal court. Most of the charges filed with the EEOC result in Right to Sue notices because the EEOC has to allocate its limited resources in a manner that will have the most dramatic effect on federal employment laws. Most state agencies follow a similar process when a claim is brought under state employment laws. In a recent National Enforcement Plan the EEOC highlighted some of the areas where it will focus its efforts in coming years. These areas include "cases involving repeated and/or egregious discrimination, including harassment, or facially discriminatory policies," as well as "challenges to broad-based employment practices affecting many employees or applicants, such as cases alleging patterns of discrimination in hiring, lay-offs, job mobility, including 'glass-ceiling' cases and/or pay."

Labor Law

CHAPTER 3

Overview of Traditional Labor Law

This is where it all began. The entire labor and employment field can trace its roots back to attorneys practicing in the traditional labor relations area. While modern employment law didn't begin to flourish in the legal arena until the 1970s and 1980s, the roots of traditional labor law go back to the late 19th century. After the formative decades of the 1920s and 1930s, labor law took off with the passage of the National Labor Relations Act (also known as "the Wagner Act," after its author, Senator Robert Wagner) in 1935. This piece of New Deal legislation, enacted in the context of frequently violent battles over union recognition, was intended to promote collective bargaining as a counterbalance to the inherent inequity in bargaining power between individual workers and management.

In the years since the enactment of landmark federal labor statutes like the NLRA and the Labor Management Relations Act of 1947 (the Taft-Hartley Act), attorneys have been battling it out from opposite sides of this practice area. In one corner, labor or union-side attorneys represent the workers' right to organize and bargain collectively. In the other corner, management-side attorneys represent companies seeking to protect their right to make independent business decisions.

Between labor and management, a deep divide

According to many traditional labor attorneys, this polarization between the two sides of the labor-management line is extreme and there is little crossover. Tim Emert, a longtime management-side attorney who began his career representing unions, has known lawyers who have made the switch from the labor side to the management side, but notes that starting out on the management side and then switching over to labor is a rare career move. When considering a career in the field of traditional labor law, this polarization should be kept in mind. It is important to spend some time thinking about which side of this divide your personal philosophy and politics fall.

Statutory Framework

Federal labor laws dominate the traditional labor relations area, although state labor laws may also be important when working with public-sector unions (government employees). Under either set of laws, labor attorneys tackle a wide variety of issues during all phases of union-management relationships.

Sections 7 and 8 of the NLRA

In the federal arena, the cornerstones of the union-management relationship are sections 7 and 8 of the National Labor Relations Act. These provisions are enforced by the National Labor Relations Board (NLRB). Section 7 gives employees the right to organize and negotiate collectively with the employer regarding the employees' terms and conditions of work, including wages, hours, discipline policy, vacation time and many other aspects of the employment relationship. The union's representation of the employees usually results in a "collective bargaining agreement," a contract between the employees/union and the employer controlling the terms and conditions of employment. Section 7 specifically provides that "employees shall have the right to self-organization, to form, join or assist labor organizations, to bargain collectively through representatives of their own choosing and to engage in concerted activities for the purpose of collective bargaining or other mutual aid or protection." Examples of protected concerted activities include lawful picketing, boycotting and strikes. The Taft-Hartley Act later amended section 7 to provide that employees also have the right to refrain from engaging in any of the concerted activities described in this section. This latter provision was added to protect employees from being coerced into participating in union organizing activity or membership.

Unfair labor practices

Section 8 of the NLRA lists "unfair labor practices" which, if engaged in by employers or unions, result in a violation of employees' protected section 7 rights. One of the fundamental unfair labor practices for employers under section 8 is interference with employees' protected section 7 rights or concerted activities. Examples of this kind of practice include forbidding employees who favor a union from soliciting other employees' support during non-working time or threatening employees that the employer will close down if a union is elected as a bargaining representative. This type of interference violation is illustrated by the landmark case of Republic Aviation Corp v. NLRB, 324 U.S. 793 (1945). In Republic Aviation, the employer had a broad no-solicitation rule that prohibited its employees from discussing union representation on company time or advertising for a union in any way. Two employees of the company wore union badges to show their support for a union and were terminated when they refused to take them off. The case was heard by the NLRB and then appealed up to the U.S. Supreme Court, which held that the broad no-solicitation rule violated the employees' section 7 rights and that the discharge of the employees for their support of the union constituted an unfair labor practice.

Another common unfair labor practice for employers is a failure to bargain with a properly certified union. For example, in NLRB v. A-1 King Size Sandwiches, Inc., 732 F.2d 872 (11th Cir. 1984), the court found that the employer had violated the duty to bargain in good faith because, even after numerous bargaining sessions over the course of a year, the employer only agreed to insignificant union demands like bulletin boards and union access to the employees. Throughout the bargaining sessions the employer demanded that it retain all control over the substantive terms and conditions of employment such as wages and hours. The court found that the employer was simply engaging in "surface bargaining" and not negotiating with the union in good faith. Aside from interference with section 7 rights or failure to bargain in good faith, other unfair labor practices include discriminating against employees based on either their membership in a union or their involvement in NLRB proceedings against the employer.

Many of the unfair labor practices that can be committed by employers have a counterpart on the union side. Unions must also bargain in good faith and refrain from interfering with or coercing employees with regard to the concerted activities listed in section 7. Examples of unlawful interference on the part of a union include unrealistic election campaign promises about increased benefits if a union is elected or threats against employees who don't join the union. In addition to the unfair labor practices that limit both sides, there are some unfair labor practices that uniquely limit union activity. For example, strikes to force a company to discharge an employee who has not joined the union constitute an unfair labor practice. Another unfair labor practice by a union is a "secondary boycott" in which a union boycotts one employer simply to get that company to stop doing business with the company that the union really has a dispute with.

Who watches the unions?

You might wonder who is keeping an eye on the unions and employers. From the very beginning, the NLRB has been charged with the task of keeping both employers and unions in line with federal labor laws.

The NLRB: labor-management referee

The National Labor Relations Board enforces the NLRA and protects employees' section 7 rights by administering union representation elections and investigating unfair labor practice charges. This agency of the federal government is like a referee in a heavyweight boxing match whose job is to get between the boxers and make sure the fight is fair. The NLRB has offices all across the country whose main role is to investigate and adjudicate unfair labor practice charges and administer representation elections to determine whether a union is entitled to be the exclusive bargaining representative for a company's employees. At the very top, the NLRB consists of a board of five members who are appointed by the president and are responsible for adjudicating disputes as to NLRA jurisdiction, union representation and unfair labor practices. The board could be compared to the U.S. Supreme Court in its own realm because it actually hears a very small number of cases; most of the work of the NLRB is carried out by subordinate officials and NLRB staff all across the country.

Investigation and adjudication

The general counsel, appointed by the president, is the prosecutorial arm of the NLRB. The general counsel is independent from the board and is charged with the task of investigating and prosecuting unfair labor practice charges and related violations of the NLRA, as well as with the general supervision of NLRB field offices. Either an employer or a union initiates the adjudication process by filing a "charge" with the NLRB. The NLRB's regional office investigates the charge to determine whether there is a valid claim. If the claim has merit, the regional director who heads the office issues a "complaint." Once the complaint is filed, an NLRB lawyer from the general counsel's office will prosecute the case before an NLRB administrative law judge on behalf of the party who filed the complaint. As in civil litigation, however, most charges or complaints are settled before they actually reach a hearing. According to the NLRB, of the roughly 35,000 charges filed each year, approximately one-third are found to have merit, and more than 90 percent of those claims are settled.

If an unfair labor practice complaint does reach a hearing, the process is much less formal than an actual civil trial because there is no pre-hearing discovery and the federal rules of evidence are not strictly applied. After a hearing, the administrative law judge, or ALJ, issues a decision that will be recommended for approval by the NLRB board members. If any party wants to appeal the recommended decision, the NLRB board members will accept written briefs on the matter before making a final decision. If no party objects to the ALJ's recommended decision it will become a final order automatically. However, many of these disputes end up in federal court because the losing party can appeal a final order to the U.S. Court of Appeals for that circuit. Moreover, because the board's order is not self-fulfilling, the NLRB must petition the Court of Appeals for enforcement of the order.

Nature of Practice and Attorneys' Roles

The union-management relationship – and where the lawyers come in

The union-management relationship traditionally begins when a labor union solicits a company's employees to choose that union as their exclusive bargaining representative. At this stage management lawyers might be called in to advise the employer on how to lawfully limit the union's access to employees and prevent employees from soliciting or distributing union material during working time. The union must obtain "authorization cards" from about 30 percent of the employees in the appropriate "bargaining unit" in order to force an election. The bargaining unit is the group of employees with common job characteristics who will be represented by the union. For example, the checkers at a grocery store or truck drivers for a delivery company could make up an appropriate bargaining unit. (Note that the actual list of factors used by the NLRB to determine what is an appropriate bargaining unit is quite detailed.) The authorization cards gathered by the interested union simply state that the employee wants the union to be its bargaining representative with the company.

Once the union submits the authorization cards to the NLRB and petitions for a "representation election," management lawyers usually serve as the employer's representative before the NLRB to contest the authorization cards if the employer believes they were obtained improperly, through coercion or by other unlawful methods. If the NLRB determines that there is a sufficient number of valid authorization cards it will either ask the parties to agree to an election or, if the parties cannot reach agreement on the details of the election, order an election after a hearing.

The collective bargaining agreement

When a majority of the employees in an appropriate bargaining unit vote to have the union serve as their representative, that union becomes the unit's exclusive representative with the employer regarding the employees' terms and conditions of employment. At this stage in the representation process, the union and the employer negotiate the collective bargaining agreement, or CBA; this contract will govern the parties' relationship over the next few years. The parties negotiate a new collective bargaining agreement when the union is first certified as the exclusive bargaining representative for the bargaining unit and whenever the term of the current CBA expires. Most collective bargaining agreements have arbitration clauses governing disputes under the contract and, once an agreement is established, labor lawyers on both sides spend a significant amount of time working on arbitrations.

Arbitration and the grievance process

An arbitration is an adversarial proceeding that resembles civil litigation but is less formal. While handling arbitrations is always an important part of working at a labor-related firm, the exact nature of arbitration varies depending on the specific industry and terms of the parties' CBA. Arbitrations are the final step in the union-management "grievance process" which is usually outlined in the CBA. A grievance is simply a dispute between the employee and/or union and the employer. For example, a grievance might involve the discharge of an employee for violating a minor employee rule like smoking on company property. Once the terminated employee complains to the union that his termination did not comply with the termination process outlined in the CBA, the grievance process begins. The first few steps of the grievance process climb their way up through various union and company officials and then, if the dispute can't be resolved, the parties end up at an arbitration hearing.

Arbitrations can be very informal proceedings that last only one hearing over a few hours. The majority of arbitrations fall into this informal category and are not even recorded on a transcript. Arbitrations in certain industries, however, more closely resemble standard civil litigation. For example, a single arbitration in the entertainment industry with unions such as the Screen Actors Guild or Directors Guild of America have formal transcripts, can involve dozens of hearings and last the better part of a year. The details of the arbitration process, such as the procedure for filing grievances, the selection and authority of the arbitrator, and the formality of the actual arbitration proceedings, are governed by the terms of each specific collective bargaining agreement and may vary dramatically. However, there are some general characteristics shared by most traditional labor arbitrations.

The arbitration usually begins with the union sending the employer a "Demand to Arbitrate," which is like the complaint in a civil trial; it provides a brief statement of the dispute and the remedy the union is seeking. The employer can then send an answer. After this initial exchange the arbitrator is usually selected by a procedure outlined in the parties' CBA. A common method for selection of an arbitrator is for a list of acceptable labor arbitrators to be sent to the union and the employer, often by the American Arbitration Association. The parties then cross off the arbitrators they object to and rank the others in order of preference. Once a mutually acceptable and available arbitrator is chosen, the parties present their case at a hearing.

Arbitration hearings generally lack the formality of civil litigation. First, the formal rules of evidence do not apply. Second, there is usually no pre-trial discovery in the form of depositions, interrogatories or requests for admissions. Accordingly, arbitration proceedings require management lawyers and their union counterparts to think on their feet, because the lawyers know very little about the other party's case or witnesses going into the hearing. Once the hearing begins, each party gives an opening statement either orally or in a written brief. The parties then present their cases through witnesses and documents.

Relevant documents like disciplinary records or timesheets are usually presented, but there are far fewer documents in an arbitration than in a civil trial because the most relevant document in an arbitration is the CBA itself. Presentation and cross-examination of witnesses also play a central role in an arbitration. After each party has presented its case it can offer a summary or closing argument. Once all of the evidence and/or written briefs have been submitted, the arbitrator closes the hearing and then makes a final judgment, usually within a time specified in the CBA. The arbitrator's award is likely to be much less formal than a court opinion, stating only the decision and brief support for that outcome.

A significant portion of labor lawyers' time is spent preparing witnesses and drafting arbitration briefs. These attorneys report that when they are preparing for an arbitration it feels just like a civil trial, with long hours and countless things to do before the big day. A large office of a management-side firm might have a couple of these arbitrations active at any given time.

Some aspects of management-side practice

In addition to arbitrations, management attorneys work with the employer on nearly every other aspect of the union-management relationship. Some management-side firms are known for their expertise in union avoidance matters and are called in before the union-management relationship even begins. If the NLRB orders a union representation election, management lawyers assist their clients in a number of ways during this contentious time. Lawyers working on union avoidance matters are likely to be involved with unfair labor practice charges because these early stages tend to be quite adversarial.

For example, in the well-known case of NLRB v. Exchange Parts, 375 U.S. 405 (1964), the union filed an unfair labor practice charge against the employer claiming that it attempted to coerce employees to vote against the union when it announced improved overtime and vacation benefits days before the representation election. Management lawyers defended the employer's action, claiming that this kind of economic change was not coercion. The NLRB found that the employer's action constituted an unfair labor practice, but the Court of Appeals disagreed and denied enforcement of the board's order. The Supreme Court later reversed, holding that the appellate court was "mistaken" in its conclusion that the employer's actions didn't interfere with the workers' protected rights.

During the election period there are bound to be unfair labor practice charges and various appeals no matter who wins the election. Management lawyers counseling a union-management relationship are also likely to encounter unfair labor practice charges more frequently. Apart from unfair labor practice charges, management attorneys represent employers in proceedings before the NLRB and similar state agencies. According to most management-side attorneys, however, practicing at a large management-side firm will likely involve working for employers that are already unionized. Therefore, these election disputes, unfair labor practice charges and other NLRB hearings will not be very common. Bernard Gold, a partner at the firm of Proskauer Rose LLP who works opposite some of the most powerful entertainment unions in the country, says that arbitrations and the administration of the collective bargaining agreement usually form the largest portion of traditional labor work at large management-side firms.

If not involved in the CBA negotiation directly, management attorneys usually help formulate bargaining strategies and offer negotiation training for the company officials sitting at the bargaining table. Management lawyers also help employers respond to information requests that might be exchanged as the parties prepare for negotiations. When a dispute arises that cannot be settled at the bargaining table, unions often resort to strikes, pickets and boycotts to exert economic pressure against the employer. During these turbulent times, management attorneys advise employers how they might legally respond to such actions and formulate ways to keep the business running until the dispute is settled. Management-side lawyers are also often involved in civil litigation arising from strikes, boycotts or other breaches of the collective bargaining agreement.

Work specific to union lawyers

According to many union-side lawyers, working on the side of labor requires an incredible amount of flexibility because attorneys must juggle such a variety of issues – from standard litigation to dealing with arrests of union officers engaged in a civil disobedience protest. While union lawyers handle a wide scope of matters, the work tends to break down into two general types that mirror the work done by their peers on the management side: (1) adversarial matters, and (2) general advising. The division between the two categories is fuzzy at times and the amount of time a given firm or lawyer spends on adversarial matters versus general advising depends on the nature of clients' needs and the type of work an individual lawyer prefers.

Adversarial matters include arbitration, election contests, unfair labor practice charges, filing or defending actions before the NLRB, and standard civil litigation. Preparing for and handling arbitrations takes up a significant portion of union attorneys' time, just as it does for lawyers on the management side. Much of this work is focused toward settlement because most grievances are settled prior to an actual arbitration. One union attorney who reports that arbitrations are a major part of her practice estimates that only about 10 percent of grievances actually go to arbitration. Another adversarial matter commonly encountered by union lawyers involve requests for information from employers. Union attorneys send information requests in order to find out more about how the employer operates and to get an accurate picture of the employer's financial position. These requests that the parties send back and forth are like discovery requests. Disputes over how much information an employer or union is required to produce often result in unfair labor practice charges.

In addition to participating in arbitrations and NLRB proceedings, labor-side attorneys might be in court for different kinds of civil litigation, some related to and some completely independent from the union-management relationship. These civil cases commonly involve breaches of the collective bargaining agreement and/or collective action issues such as the legality of certain strikes, pickets or boycotts. Union lawyers also litigate cases in which the union defends charges that it discriminated against its own employees or breached its duty of fair representation to an individual union member. Labor lawyers emphasize that much of their litigation work is spent researching and drafting dispositive motions such as motions to dismiss or motions for summary judgment. As in most forms of litigation, actually trying a case is the exception rather than the rule.

Union lawyers also dispense advice to their clients. Such counsel might be related to adversarial matters like unfair labor practice charges and arbitration. Or it might involve the legality of strikes, protests, boycotts and other forms of collective action. Union lawyers also provide assistance during collective bargaining negotiation and lead training sessions for unions and their members on topics ranging from how to be shop steward to how to file a grievance.

ON THE JOB

Psst...
Need a Change in Venue?

Use the Internet's most targeted job search tools for law professionals.

Vault Law Job Board

The most comprehensive and convenient job board for law professionals. Target your search by area of law, function, and experience level, and find the job openings that you want. No surfing required.

VaultMatch Resume Database

Vault takes match-making to the next level: post your resume and customize your search by area of law, experience and more. We'll match job listings with your interests and criteria and e-mail them directly to your inbox.

Employment Law

CHAPTER 4

Management/Defense-side Practice

Law firms that represent the interests of management/employers (otherwise known as defense side) come in all shapes and sizes. At the larger end of the spectrum are the giant national and international law firms with labor and employment departments packed with hundreds of attorneys. Firms that are well known for their employment practices include Paul, Hastings, Janofsky & Walker; Morgan, Lewis & Bockius; and Proskauer Rose, to name just a few. In the middle of the spectrum are national or regional law firms specializing in employment matters, such as Littler Mendelson or Fisher & Phillips. At the smaller end of the spectrum are "boutique" employment firms with a handful of attorneys that specialize in employment defense matters. Examples of these firms include Swerdlow Florence Sanchez Swerdlow and Wimmer in Los Angeles; Benetar Bernstein Schair & Stein in New York; and Kauff McClain & McGuire, with offices in New York and San Francisco. These firms may also work on the management side of traditional labor matters.

Employment boutiques

Lean staffing and early responsibility

At smaller firms or employment boutiques, the emphasis is on litigation, most of which is likely to involve single- or multi-plaintiff lawsuits rather than large class actions. The lower billing rates at smaller firms attract such single-plaintiff work because there is often less at stake in these cases. While some small firms do handle class actions, those complex cases tend to be the exception rather than the rule. New associates at these firms are also likely to encounter smaller matters such as worker's compensation or unemployment benefit disputes. This aspect of small firm practice may be a blessing for new associates because single-plaintiff cases and smaller matters are leanly staffed and usually provide ample opportunities for substantive litigation work, like taking depositions and drafting significant motions.

While much of the substantive work is comparable, the pay scale and other amenities associated with some large firms are not likely to be found at these smaller employment boutiques. The salaries for new hires at small firms generally fall in the $50,000 to $85,000 range depending on the geographic market. On the other hand, the billable hour requirements are normally not as demanding as those at large firms. While attorneys at small firms may enjoy early litigation experience, a litigation-centered practice will probably not provide the same opportunities to work on transactional or corporate-related matters offered by a larger, departmentalized firm. A junior associate at a small firm should also be prepared to undertake more administrative duties (such as filing, mailing and editing documents) than his or her peers at larger firms, which tend to be staffed with more assistants and paralegals.

Large law firms

Variations in the employment department model

There is no uniform structure for employment departments at large firms. Employment lawyers at some large firms may spend up to 80 percent of their time on litigation-related matters, while attorneys elsewhere might handle more corporate and transactional work and leave the actual employment litigation to the firm's general litigation department. According to one employment associate at a big firm, "Sometimes large firms' rate structures are such that employment litigation (which may be small dollars) goes elsewhere, making it far more likely that employment lawyers will work on corporate deals." The attorney adds that, "As rates go up, the amount of employment litigation at large firms decreases. Notably, this is a corollary to the idea that younger associates generally get more hands-on experience in an employment practice than in other areas (the cases must be staffed leanly because the amount in controversy is usually modest.)" At the same time, other large-firm associates report that litigation and litigation-related counseling continues to make up the bulk of their practice.

Big-name clients and big cases

At large law firms, new attorneys find sophisticated work and a high-profile and stable client base. One advantage to working with a base of regular clients is the opportunity to develop long-term relationships of trust and confidence. Morgan Lewis associate Sarah Bouchard finds the ongoing relations with firm clients one of the "most rewarding" aspects of her practice. Junior associates at large employment firms are also likely to encounter a mix of single-plaintiff actions and large class actions. As the billing rates at most large firms skyrocket to compensate for the increases in associate salaries, these firms are increasingly shifting their litigation focus to class actions that generate a substantial number of billable hours. Smaller, more tightly-staffed cases may be harder to come by at a large firm; this difficulty, according to an employment lawyer at a top firm, is a constant issue for associates.

In spite of this economic reality, many large firms realize that small single-plaintiff actions are essential for training top-flight homegrown associates, so they try to ensure that a number of smaller cases are available for new lawyers. Regardless of where you decide to practice, you should make sure that you will be able to work on some single- or multi-plaintiff suits early in your career because they provide the greatest opportunity to handle important aspects of a case.

With higher salaries, higher expectations

On the compensation side, large firms are at the pinnacle of the legal pay scale. Salary wars between firms during the dot-com boom have resulted in first-year salaries ranging from $95,000 to $135,000 depending on the geographic market. Before the dot-com bubble burst, year-end bonuses at these firms reached anywhere from $10,000 to $50,000 and beyond. More recently, however, most large firms have begun to delicately suggest that big bonuses are a thing of the past. Large firms also frequently provide a smorgasbord of other benefits that can include health club memberships, discounted theater and sports tickets, fancy attorney dining rooms – even biweekly massages!

These perks and benefits do come at a price; new associates at large firms are expected to work very hard and be extremely efficient. According to an employment litigator at a respected national firm, young lawyers coming into a large firm should be prepared to work extremely hard and demonstrate their value to the firm within their first year because "At $125,000 a year what you bring to the equation is youth, energy and a healthy fear of failure." Minimum billable hour requirements at most large firms climb well above 2,000 hours. Moreover, the average number of hours billed by junior associates is likely to be a few hundred hours more than that minimum. These numbers may not mean much to you in law school time, but the 200-hour difference between 1,900 and 2,100 billable hours can mean the difference between enjoying weekends at the beach or spending them in the office. Several contacts at large firms suggest that the "ever-increasing focus" on billable hours, more than the actual number of hours required, is the most frustrating aspect of their practice. When considering various employment options you should analyze all of these factors before making any final decisions.

Plaintiffs' Counsel

Representing the underdog

If you have a passion for civil rights and like to root for the underdog, you might find working on the plaintiffs' side of the employment bar a good fit. While plaintiffs aren't always the underdog, many plaintiffs' lawyers report that they at least feel like the underdog most of the time. Plaintiffs' side attorneys encounter many unique, challenging and potentially rewarding aspects of litigation practice not experienced by their peers on the management side. The substantive nature of the work, however, is virtually identical.

Plaintiffs' lawyers represent the parties that initiate the kinds of employment litigation discussed in the last chapter, from sexual harassment to age discrimination to wage and hour litigation. Plaintiff-side practice is almost exclusively focused on litigation. The kind of counseling plaintiffs' attorneys provide entails consulting with potential clients to evaluate the merits of a case. Again, if your civil procedure class seemed like a trip to the dentist's office, employment litigation may not be the field for you. On the other hand, if the thought of standing up in front of a jury and telling your client's story excites you, there may be no better place to practice than on the plaintiffs' side of the employment bar.

Focus on smaller cases

Unlike the different sizes you find on the management/defense side, plaintiffs' firms tend to come in one size only – small. Most plaintiffs' firms are small litigation firms with a handful of attorneys who represent plaintiffs in a variety of cases. While some plaintiffs' firms specialize in employment litigation, others combine their employment practice with civil rights cases, personal injury work or other kinds of litigation. Examples of plaintiffs' firms well known for employment litigation include Rudy, Exelrod & Zieff in San Francisco and Hadsell & Stormer in Los Angeles. Because of their smaller size, plaintiffs' firms tend to have localized practices concentrated in one metropolitan area or, at most, an entire state. The mainstay of these firms are single- and multi-plaintiff actions. Larger class actions, which involve significant financial risk for plaintiffs' counsel, are usually brought by firms with expertise in class actions or by the Equal Employment Opportunity Commission. The EEOC is a major force in the world of employment law and acts essentially as the federal government's plaintiffs' firm for employment matters. (The EEOC will be discussed in more detail below.)

Sink or swim training

At private plaintiffs' firms, the focus on smaller cases allows new lawyers to work on significant matters early in their careers. Brian Soriano, an employment litigator at Goldstein, Gellman, Melbostad, Gibson & Harris LLP, suggests that as a junior attorney at a plaintiffs' firm you will probably get substantial responsibility on a case – even before you think you're ready. This "sink or swim" method of training is common at plaintiffs' firms which need associates to be competent litigators early on because they just don't have time to slowly train new attorneys and bring them up through the ranks. Not only do junior plaintiffs' attorneys frequently enjoy more responsibility than their counterparts at large management firms, but they also are likely to have greater client contact.

Holding the client's hand

Plaintiffs' lawyers work closely with clients who may feel victimized and at times be very emotional. The close relationships that often develop between employment discrimination plaintiffs and their attorneys can require a certain amount of "client management" or "hand-holding" (as some lawyers like to call it), and at such times plaintiffs' lawyers may assume a role closer to counselor than litigator. Plaintiffs' attorneys also have to deal with clients' mood swings that range from disenchantment with the litigation to holding onto an unreasonable settlement position because they are so emotionally entangled in the case. These aspects of the attorney-client relationship come at a much earlier stage to attorneys on the plaintiffs' side than to defense-side lawyers. Associates at plaintiffs' firms often have significant interaction with clients in their first few years of practice, while partners are usually the main contact with clients on the management side and actual interaction with corporate clients may not trickle far down the ranks. Many lawyers find the early responsibility, close client contact and opportunity to litigate a ton of cases attractive aspects of plaintiff-side practice.

More food for thought

On the other hand, the plaintiffs' side of the bar offers fewer opportunities for young attorneys to obtain practical training from attentive senior litigators. Plaintiffs' side litigators tend to be independent types who aren't in the business of building a law firm full of well-trained associates. Even when you find an opportunity on the plaintiffs' side it will not be nearly as lucrative in the beginning as starting out on the management side. Entry-level associate positions on the plaintiffs' side are usually in the $55,000 to $75,000 range, while starting salaries on the management side may be twice that amount. In addition, more senior plaintiffs' attorneys have to deal with all of the risks associated with contingent fee arrangements that are the foundation of plaintiffs' side work. Contingency-based fees can, of course, prove very lucrative, but they involve a degree of financial risk that management-side lawyers don't usually have to deal with.

The EEOC

As the agency responsible for enforcing federal employment discrimination laws, the Equal Employment Opportunity Commission might be considered the biggest plaintiffs' firm of them all. EEOC lawyers tend to serve two functions. First, they serve as in-house counsel for the investigative arm of the agency. In this capacity EEOC lawyers might take complaints or investigate claims. Second, EEOC attorneys serve as trial lawyers in federal court, prosecuting the employment cases that could not be settled by the parties voluntarily through the EEOC's conciliation process. The cases actually tried by the EEOC tend be higher profile cases and provide EEOC lawyers with the opportunity to litigate opposite some of the best private practice employment litigators in the country. Such unique litigation experiences are among the reasons that positions at the EEOC are in short supply. Another reason is that the EEOC's ability to hire lawyers is directly tied to its general budget, which must be approved by Congress.

The starting salary at the EEOC is around $42,000 (GS-11 level) but, according to the agency's web site, a new lawyer's salary can reach nearly $83,000 (GS-15 level) in about four years. Because the General Schedule pay rates are adjusted geographically, the actual salaries in some regions may be higher.

Labor Law

CHAPTER 5

Representing Management

Large firms serving large companies

While there are management-side firms in the small and mid-size range, a large percentage of attorneys that represent management practice at large national or international law firms. Employers that have the most at stake with respect to labor relations tend to be large companies that can afford to pay the higher costs associated with large firm representation. These enormous firms are the same big firms discussed in the employment litigation section, and an associate's life at one of these firms is subject to the same pros and cons of big-firm practice. On the other hand, because traditional labor relations cases might not involve substantial sums of money, some of this work likely goes to smaller management-side firms with lower billing rates.

In addition to law firm positions, many corporations have in-house counsel who specialize in labor relations. These positions are generally reserved for experienced labor lawyers, so don't expect to land one of these jobs fresh out of law school.

Representing Labor

Union boutiques

Labor-side attorneys usually practice at boutique-size firms committed specifically to union representation. These firms can range from a few attorneys to a few dozen, but even the largest union firms are dwarfed in size by their management-side counterparts. Union firms do not have the fanciest offices around and are usually without the support staff you might find on the management side. This requires union lawyers to engage in a fair amount of administrative work and other "non-lawyering" activities that many of their peers on the management side aren't bothered with.

Starting salaries on the union side are usually in the $45,000 to $80,000 range, depending on the geographic market. While the salaries at union firms may be lower than those at management firms, so are the billable hour requirements. Another upside to union-side practice is that these firms tend to specialize in union representation and do not have the management side's overlap between labor and employment law, so someone dedicated to traditional labor relations work can focus on those matters.

In-house at a union

A mix of labor and employment law

A union-side firm isn't the only place to practice as a union lawyer. The largest unions usually have in-house legal departments and many union lawyers work in-house at a union itself. An in-house position at a union operates much like the in-house corporate counsel positions discussed below, but there are some aspects unique to union lawyers. Only the largest unions have in-house legal positions; average-size unions are represented by firms specializing in labor representation.

In-house union counsel must be excellent communicators able to deal with difficult people in emotional situations. In-house attorneys will also likely practice in both arenas of traditional labor law and general employment law. Unlike private practice, these attorneys don't get to choose their clients because they must represent the individual members of the union in addition to the union itself.

When representing individuals, in-house union lawyers encounter all types of employment issues, including contract disputes, discrimination claims and other violations of state employment laws. When representing the union, these attorneys are involved in organization efforts, collective bargaining negotiations, arbitrations and the various NLRB or state agency proceedings discussed in the last chapter. In-house lawyers do not always represent the union themselves and may coordinate representation from outside law firms. Union counsel also conduct training for the union staff engaged in CBA negotiation and arbitration and for other union members. Preparing publications to keep members informed on relevant legal issues is also a common task for in-house union lawyers.

In addition to representing the union on labor relations issues, these in-house attorneys also counsel their clients on the broad range of issues that arise for any business entity. Unions are employers like any other business, and in-house lawyers advise their clients on the whole spectrum of employment issues that arise in the employment setting. For example, unions can be sued under Title VII or similar state laws for discrimination, and in-house attorneys are frequently involved in defending the union in these cases. Segments of a union's employees, like the clerical employees, might be unionized themselves and the in-house attorney would be involved in all aspects of the relationship between the "inside" union and the employer-union in its management capacity. Union counsel also advise their clients on business-related issues that may include real estate, insurance or tax concerns. Again, in-house attorneys may work on these matters personally or farm out the work to outside counsel depending on the complexity of the matter and the degree of specialization required.

Satisfaction beyond salary

The salary range for in-house positions is usually slightly lower than for firm practice. However, although these positions tend to pay less than firm positions, in-house labor counsel commonly report that being such an integral part of the labor movement brings a sense of job satisfaction that might not be found elsewhere.

THE NLRB

NLRB attorneys investigate and prosecute unfair labor practice charges before administrative law judges, the NLRB itself, federal appeals courts and even the U.S. Supreme Court. All of this action comes quickly to NLRB attorneys because matters are leanly staffed and there are plenty of small matters for new attorneys to work on. In addition to litigation-related activity, NLRB lawyers counsel the agency and its regional offices regarding all aspects of the NLRB's work.

According to an NLRB recruiting manual, many law school graduates start at the GS-11 level, with a salary of around $42,000. If they "develop as expected," they could reach a salary of $60,000 (GS-13 level) within two years.

In-house Employment Counsel

CHAPTER 6

While the thrill of actually litigating cases never gets old for some lawyers, many labor and employment attorneys prefer the counseling aspects of management-side practice and would rather spend their time providing preventive advice and guidance. After gaining a substantial base of litigation experience, some of these counseling-oriented lawyers leave firm practice to become "in-house" employment lawyers for large corporations. In-house positions play an important part in employment practice and you should be familiar with them if you plan to enter the field in any capacity.

The Work of an In-house Attorney

In-house employment lawyers frequently rave about their jobs. They enjoy flexible schedules and a great deal of independence in their work. They don't have senior attorneys breathing down their necks about a memo that was due yesterday because they are usually among the senior attorneys in their workplace. In-house lawyers also don't have the billable hour requirements that torment lawyers working at traditional law firms. Perhaps the most rewarding part of an in-house lawyer's practice is the opportunity to become intimately involved in the daily life of a single business entity. In-house lawyers usually play an indispensable part in the decision-making process at their companies.

The actual title of these in-house positions differs from company to company but it is usually some form of "assistant general counsel" position stationed in the legal or human resource department of large corporations. The nature of an in-house position will vary with the size of the company and the industry in which it operates. For example, an in-house employment lawyer working at a heavily unionized grocery store chain will spend much more time on labor relations issues like collective bargaining agreement administration than would an in-house employment lawyer at a software company that has very few, if any, unionized employees. While the actual substance of the work may differ, the practice of in-house employment lawyers tends to fall into one of two general categories: (1) day-to-day counseling, and (2) managing labor or employment cases that are actually litigated by outside counsel.

Day-to-day counseling

On the day-to-day counseling matters, in-house employment lawyers essentially take the counseling aspects of firm practice and turn it into a full-time endeavor. Counseling usually takes up only a small percentage of an employment lawyer's time at a traditional firm, whereas counseling clients on the labor and employment issues that arise in the workplace makes up the vast majority of an in-house lawyer's workload. In-house attorneys are constantly on the phone or sending e-mails back and forth to their "clients," who are usually company executives, managers or human resources professionals. The substantive labor or employment issues that in-house lawyers encounter are the same ones faced by law firm attorneys. On larger scale matters, in-house lawyers might advise high-level executives on the legal issues associated with a mass layoff or a merger. Smaller employment matters might include investigating sexual harassment charges, advising human resources professionals on appropriate forms of discipline for a certain employee and evaluating the type of accommodations or leave an employee is entitled to under the ADA or FMLA.

In-house attorneys also conduct training sessions for employees and human resources professionals on discrimination, harassment and employee benefit issues. If the company an in-house lawyer works for has large segments of its workforce unionized the lawyer might help negotiate collective bargaining agreements, which usually expire every three to four years. They would also advise their clients on the day-to-day administration of the CBA by answering questions such as whether changes in the company's policies need to be discussed with the union. Despite their best efforts to avoid litigation, however, in-house employment lawyers often become intimately involved in actual labor and employment litigation.

Overseeing outside litigators

In-house employment lawyers hire outside attorneys to represent the company when it becomes involved in litigation arising out of the employment relationship. These cases can range from Title VII discrimination claims to wage and hour class actions brought under state laws similar to the FLSA. In-house lawyers discuss litigation strategy and settlement options and review motions filed on behalf of the company. They also give outside litigators guidance on where to find important documents or which employees need to be contacted regarding a particular issue in a case. They attend mediations and settlement conferences as well as depositions of important parties or witnesses in some cases. The actual amount of involvement an in-house lawyer has on a given case depends on the nature of the case and how many cases the attorney has active at a given time. If an in-house lawyer's company has 20 different suits pending at the same time, the attorney will probably not be too involved in a small FMLA benefits case but might be intimately involved in a wage and hour class action involving hundreds of plaintiffs and millions of dollars in potential damages. In-house employment lawyers are also responsible for keeping company executives and human resources professionals informed on the status of pending litigation.

Financial Rewards

If, after becoming a proficient employment litigator, you manage to find an in-house position, you will likely be handsomely rewarded. While in-house employment lawyers may not make as much as partners at large management-side law firms, their salaries are usually somewhere in the $100,000 to $200,000 range. According to Altman Weil Publications, Inc.'s 2000 Law Department Compensation Benchmarking Survey, the 1999 national average salary for regular in-house lawyers was $108,826, while "High-Level Specialist" lawyers raked in an average of $140,566. In addition to regular paychecks, in-house counsel may also be rewarded with stock options that can substantially boost their compensation package depending on the financial health of the company. The risks of a benefit package that is heavy on stock options and light on salary is one aspect of in-house practice that must be weighed before any seasoned litigator decides to leave firm practice and head in-house.

A Day in the Life

CHAPTER 7

A Day in the Life of An Employment Litigator

Theresa Whitman

Associate, Employment Law Department
Paul, Hastings, Janofsky & Walker LLP

7:45 a.m.: Arrive at office; checked e-mail, voice mail and a few faxes.

8:00 a.m.: Edit an outline prepared within the firm that summarizes recent significant California employment law cases.

8:15 a.m.: Prepare to attend ex-parte hearing regarding an application by plaintiff to shorten time to file and have the court hear a motion to compel further response to interrogatories.

9:30 a.m.: Attend a hearing with a partner regarding cross-motions for summary judgment. The plaintiff's motion was denied and our client's motion was granted, resulting in a judgment against plaintiff on his entire complaint.

11:00 a.m.: Meet with senior associate to discuss preparing opposition to a motion to compel further responses to interrogatories to be heard the next day (the same matter on which I was in court earlier in the day for the ex-parte hearing).

11:30 a.m.: Prepare opposition to motion to compel further interrogatory responses.

12:30 p.m.: Review documents and deposition transcripts to prepare to attend expert witness deposition.

1:00 p.m.: Eat lunch on the way to expert witness deposition.

1:30 p.m.: Attend expert witness deposition.

4:00 p.m.: Continue to prepare opposition to motion to compel further interrogatory responses and supporting documentation.

7:00 p.m.: Meet with senior associate to receive feedback on opposition to motion to compel.

7:30 p.m.: Leave office and head home.

A Day in the Life of a Plaintiffs' Lawyer

Thomas Duckworth

Partner
Otis Canli & Duckworth LLP

8:00 a.m.: Meet with other lawyers at the firm to discuss the 70 or so intake calls we received in the last month regarding potential claims. We discuss the merits of each case and whether the firm should agree to represent the plaintiff(s).

10:15 a.m.: Draft discovery requests in a case involving promissory fraud regarding an executive's employment.

1:15 p.m.: Call some of the potential clients discussed in the morning "intake" meeting in order to get some more information and clarify questions we had about their specific situation.

1:45 p.m.: Call some of the potential clients to inform them that we would not be able to represent them.

2:30 p.m.: Hold consultation meeting with a potential client to review a severance agreement the potential client was about to enter into with his employer.

3:45 p.m.: Draft more discovery requests for a promissory fraud case.

5:20 p.m.: Research validity of an arbitration agreement in a California wage and hour class action.

6:30 p.m.: Head home.

A Day in the Life of a Management Attorney

Howard L. Ganz

Partner
Proskauer Rose LLP

8:15 a.m.: I arrive at the office; check my voice mail (already two messages) and e-mail. I begin attempting to get through index of cases recently filed in local federal and state courts to see if any deserve attention. I also review *Sports Business Daily* for recent developments, spotting a brief reference to SDNY decision in case brought by football player who was injured by penalty flag thrown by referee and asked litigation support office to secure copy of decision.

8:45 a.m.: Attend an internal meeting to plan an annual CLE program we run for sports law clients (what subjects to cover, who should be presenters, what did we learn from evaluation submitted with respect to last year's program).

9:30 a.m.: Prepare for and attend meeting at sports client to discuss status of collective bargaining negotiations and future strategy.

12:30 p.m.: Return to office and have lunch at desk. Check voice mail and e-mail and respond to messages. Begin to review responses to interrogatories and document requests in case in which the former general counsel of the baseball umpires' union that was decertified in NLRB election alleges that our employer-client tortiously interfered with his retainer agreement with that union. Confer with a colleague who has drafted responses.

1:45 p.m.: Telephone call with entertainment industry client with respect to completion of EEO-1 forms.

2:00 p.m.: Review the transcript of most recent hearing in long-running arbitration brought by baseball players' union. Begin work on outlines of testimony for witnesses to be called.

3:00 p.m.: Telephone call with an adversary to discuss possible settlement of case involving allegedly wrongful termination of former executive at insurance industry client. Telephone call with my client to report progress. Send e-mails to other lawyers working on matter to give them an update.

3:15 p.m.: Review notes on interviews conducted in connection with investigation into alleged misconduct of senior executive at entertainment industry client. Edit draft report of findings and conclusions.

4:30 p.m.: Meet with first-year associate to provide interim evaluation; prepare memo summarizing conversation.

5:15 p.m.: Telephone call with lawyers from NBA with respect to interpretation of collective bargaining agreement with players' union.

5:30 p.m.: Telephone call with adversary in a case in which we are representing executive of publishing industry client who seeks payment under "change in control" agreement with former employer. We discuss possible mediation of the dispute.

5:45 p.m.: I review recent decision involving injured football player; prepare memo summarizing decision for various sports clients.

6:30 p.m.: Catch up on e-mails.

6:45 p.m.: I review draft of press release to be issued by sports client with respect to ongoing collective bargaining negotiations. Make proposed edits, fax edited version back to the client and follow up with a telephone call to the client.

7:15 p.m.: Attend party honoring senior human resources official of broadcasting company client upon his retirement.

10:00 p.m.: I go home. Check office voice mails and e-mails, deciding that all can wait until morning.

A Day in the Life of a Union Attorney

Ariana R. Levinson

Associate
Holguin & Garfield, APLC

9:15 a.m.: Arrive at the office, check e-mail and get situated.

9:30 a.m.: Research the fairly obscure issue of whether an employer's use of joint union-employer letterhead without union consent is grounds for an unfair labor practice charge.

11:20 a.m.: Take care of some administrative work, organizing research files and looking at mail from over the weekend.

11:40 a.m.: Review fax regarding a grievance that the union is pursuing to arbitration to make sure arbitration demand was amended. Review voluntary NLRB notices of dismissal.

12:15 p.m.: Hold phone conference with NLRB agent. NLRB is filing a complaint on an information request charge against an employer and informs me that the employer had filed an information request charge against the union. Discuss the issue with the partner on the case and e-mail our client.

12:40 p.m.: I call the business representative of a client to discuss a protest being planned that may involve some civil disobedience.

1:00 p.m.: Eat lunch at desk while reading *Daily Journal* and the latest issue of BNA's *Labor Relations Reporting Manual Update*.

1:45 p.m.: Draft answer to a tort complaint-in-intervention filed against union because of an injury to a trucker by a member dispatched from a hiring hall.

2:00 p.m.: Call a client to discuss prior settlement agreement.

2:05 p.m.: Research the proper method of service of summons on a [John] Doe defendant and complete a draft of answer.

6:00 p.m.: Leave the office.

A Day in the Life of an In-House Employment Attorney

Mia Montpas

Assistant General Counsel, Human Resources, Labor and Benefits
Honeywell International

8:15 a.m.: Handle a race discrimination allegation from a senior-level employee. Assess the issues and ultimately determine to bring in an independent investigator to handle. (Often I would investigate such an allegation myself, although this issue involves a situation where I am a witness so I cannot do it myself.)

10:30 a.m.: Counsel a human resource officer regarding a termination in Mexico of an employee for an integrity breach with a customer.

11:00 a.m.: Revise a letter to a pregnant employee. We're redefining her job duties due to her request to go part-time.

11:30 a.m.: Discuss a potential plant shut down of a site in South America.

1:15 p.m.: Discuss a performance management situation. Advise various human resources personnel of the need for documentation and due process (hearings, and so forth).

1:35 p.m.: Advise human resources personnel regarding an ADA and FMLA issue for an employee who had exhausted FMLA leave but still needs additional time off.

2:15 p.m.: Look at and research a short-term disability issue as it relates to an ongoing workers compensation case.

2:50 p.m.: Talk with outside counsel regarding a "whistleblower" case.

3:30 p.m.: Meet with the president about ongoing business and HR issues at a particular site.

4:10 p.m.: Discuss four ongoing grievances at one of our union sites. Selected arbitrators with the union.

4:45 p.m.: Discuss a bonus scheme for employees with HR personnel in our United Kingdom division.

5:30 p.m.: Research some sex discrimination and harassment issues for a financial employee.

6:00 p.m.: At the end of the day, I conduct performance management training for a group of managers.

GETTING HIRED

Questions to Consider

CHAPTER 8

Whose Side Are You On?

Before you start looking for jobs, it's a good idea to consider what it is that attracts you to labor and employment practice. The previous chapters have given an overview of the kinds of work labor lawyers and employment attorneys encounter and outlined some of the differences among the various practices. These differences can involve the amount of salary and the presence (or absence) of notable perks, the number of hours worked, the kind of training new associates receive, the size and nature of cases handled, the degree of responsibility and client contact afforded a junior lawyer, as well as how an attorney's personal philosophy might come into play.

If you decide to pursue a career as an employment litigator, whether on the plaintiffs' side or on the defense, you should first sit down and really think about your personal philosophy and politics. Such an exercise is perhaps even more important for labor law enthusiasts, given the wide, often hard-to-bridge, chasm that divides labor and management.

Where to Practice?

Once you decide which side of the bar you want to work for, you must consider the different places where you might practice. Are you drawn to public service or do you prefer private practice? Does the prospect of jumping right into the deep end of a case thrill you (in which case, a small plaintiffs' firm might hold special appeal), or would you rather have the longer tutelage under more experienced attorneys that larger firms usually provide? Are you equally interested in employment law and labor relations work, or do you want to concentrate in just one of those areas? Is it only the thought of actually litigating cases that keeps you slogging through all those boring transactional law school courses? Or do you relish the idea of participating on corporate deals, drafting agreements and offering guidance in order to help clients avoid adversarial nightmares?

What Qualities Will Serve You Best?

As you evaluate your career options, you would do well also to consider what assets you will bring to a labor or employment practice – assets that go beyond the credentials highlighted on your resume. Labor and employment lawyers say "intelligence, good writing skills, strong work ethic and honesty" are vital. Attention to detail is a must in order to excel, say practitioners. The ability to handle several assignments at the same time is another desirable skill. Balancing competing assignments and demands can be challenging, but, according to Sarah Bouchard, a lawyer at Morgan, Lewis & Bockius, it also makes the work "more diverse and rewarding." And to succeed in the long run, suggests a senior associate at a top firm, a lawyer must "also be able to bring in business."

In addition to these general skills, other qualities may be particularly valuable to those who practice in labor and employment law. A prospective labor or employment attorney should have a real desire to be a specialist rather than a generalist – to become a "master of that narrow field," in the words of one lawyer. Another "critical" quality mentioned by practitioners is the ability to communicate with different people in different capacities. As one associate explains, an employment lawyer, unlike a corporate attorney, deals with a wide range of people – some of whom are well-educated and high-powered, others of whom are not. The successful lawyer will be able to communicate effectively and sensitively with people at all levels, from a plant supervisor to a junior human resources officer to a financial industry CEO or the general counsel at a publicly traded company. A related attribute is sensitivity to different industries, whether blue- or white-collar, with which an attorney might come in contact. According to a lawyer at a prominent East Coast firm, this is not only a skill you bring to your practice, but also one of its rewards; dealing with such a broad range of people from their perspective is "almost a study in sociology."

Landing a Job

CHAPTER 9

General Strategies

Law school courses

Whether you are interested in practicing labor or employment law, representing management, plaintiffs or unions, the first place to start preparing for your career is the law school course catalog. The most common piece of advice from practicing attorneys: take as many labor and employment law classes as you can. It's one thing to state an interest in employment or labor law; it's another to be able to offer an interviewer a concrete demonstration of your enthusiasm.

If you are interested in employment law, whether on the plaintiff or defense side, you should take any courses at your law school that cover employment law or employment discrimination. These classes will introduce you to Title VII and the statutory framework of the employment practice. If your goal is a career in traditional labor law, look for courses that cover the National Labor Relations Act and the history of labor relations. Litigation-related courses and classes that review arbitration practice will also be helpful.

Practical experience

Because both employment practice and traditional labor law involve substantial doses of litigation and arbitration, you should take advantage of opportunities to gain practical experience in these areas. Moot court, clinical classes or judicial externships will not only provide real or simulated litigation experience, they also will show potential employers that you are really serious about litigating. Other useful experience might include working in a business's human resources department or doing union-related work. Consider applying for a summer internship or job with the government – for example, the EEOC, the NLRB or the Department of Labor.

Networking

One way to get acquainted with labor and employment firms and attorneys in your area is to join your local bar association as a student member. Nearly every sizable bar association will have a labor and employment section, and attending its events can be an invaluable way to come into contact with attorneys at firms of all sizes. Showing up as a student among practicing attorneys might seem a bit intimidating at first, but you will likely find that the lawyers you meet will be more than generous with their time and happy to answer any questions you have about the practice in general and firms in their area. Many employment litigators suggest that this is the best step a law student can take to begin networking within the employment practice.

Targeted Tips: Employment Law

Landing a job on the management/defense side

Because the practice of employment law varies from firm to firm, try to find out as much as you can about an individual firm, including the model its departments follow. For example, if you are interested in employment litigation, find out whether the attorneys in a firm's employment department handle their own litigation or whether that's left to the general litigation department while employment associates spend their time on counseling and corporate support. In general, smaller firms or boutiques are more likely to concentrate on litigation than transactional work, while employment attorneys at large firms will handle a heavy load of corporate support.

Large firms: Buff that resume

Large management-side firms usually recruit heavily on law school campuses across the country. While directly contacting these firms and expressing interest in their employment practices is never a bad idea, the main thrust of their recruiting efforts is through on-campus interviews heading up their summer associate programs. This general pattern applies to large national firms, national employment law firms and larger regional firms.

Simply because these firms may be actively recruiting law students and new attorneys doesn't mean landing a job at a large, respected management firm is an easy task. Such national firms are extremely selective, and scoring good grades at a top law school is often a prerequisite. A mid-level associate at Paul, Hastings, Janofsky & Walker suggests that "There is a grade guideline for each school which successful candidates typically meet." The "better the law school, grades, journal/law review and prior work experience, the better the chance of getting hired is." Even though "personality is also very important," you must first have the "right combination of law school and grades." One tip offered is to publish a scholarly article during school. This, notes the associate, can be "very distinguishing, especially if the student is seeking to target a particular [practice] area."

Employment boutiques: Put on your sneakers

Landing a job at a respected employment boutique may require a bit more footwork than simply showing up at your on-campus interview with a glowing resume. Unlike national or large regional firms, smaller employment firms don't recruit heavily on law school campuses, and they are more likely to require some prior litigation experience. However, with a little research and a lot of legwork you should be able to find opportunities at respected boutiques in your area. Initially you should consult your career services center, employment law professors and any practicing attorneys you know to help you locate smaller firms in your area with well-known employment practices. While you are at the career services center, ask if there are any small or mid-size firm receptions or events that may not be part of the main on-campus recruiting programs, as these are usually dominated by larger firms. Networking becomes especially valuable when seeking a job at these harder-to-find boutique firms, and you should tap into the resources offered by local bar groups.

Once you've located firms that catch your interest, contact them directly and clearly demonstrate your interest in employment law in any communications. In the first paragraph of your cover letter you should bring to their attention any employment classes you've taken, any practical litigation experience you have, like externships or law clerk positions, and any other activities that demonstrate your interest in employment law or litigation. Don't be discouraged if you send out dozens of letters and get no response. If you've done your research and are persistent, the hard work will pay off somewhere down the line. While smaller firms don't usually have the recruiting budgets for lavish summer associate programs, they will likely have some sort of law clerking program that may lead to a permanent position.

Landing a job at a plaintiffs' firm

A drive for justice

Plaintiffs' firms, like management boutiques, do not recruit heavily on law school campuses and look extremely favorably on any prior litigation experience. While it is difficult to generalize in this regard, many plaintiffs' attorneys contacted say they feel committed to the cause of helping victims of discrimination find justice and usually look for the same philosophical drive in new hires. When seeking a position at a plaintiffs' firm you should demonstrate a commitment specifically to the plaintiffs' side of the employment bar, not just employment litigation in general.

Plaintiffs' attorneys suggest that a good way to demonstrate a commitment to the plaintiffs' bar and to network with lawyers is to join an association for plaintiffs' attorneys in the employment practice. These organizations are like local bar associations, but more specialized. The most prominent association for plaintiffs' attorneys in the employment area is the National Employment Lawyers Association (NELA). Another valuable resource is the Association of Trial Lawyers of America (ATLA), the world's largest trial bar, which has an employment rights section.

Most states also have associations for litigators on the plaintiffs' side of the employment bar, such as the NELA-New York and the California Employment Lawyers Association (CELA). (A list of associations for plaintiffs' attorneys in the employment area for each state can be found on NELA's web site, at www.nela.org/about/about_affiliates.htm.) Nearly all of these associations have law student memberships with reduced fees. Taking advantage of the networking opportunities these organizations provide will help with the difficult task of finding positions on the plaintiffs' side.

Legwork and determination

Once you have located well-respected plaintiffs' firms in your area, be proactive and contact these firms directly. Again, in communicating with these firms, clearly highlight any litigation-related activity and your interest in employment practice on the plaintiffs' side of the bar. As in any area of the employment field, taking law school classes that cover Title VII and state anti-discrimination statutes is recommended because it will expose you to the general concepts in employment discrimination law and enable you to have informed discussions with practitioners. The key to finding a position on the plaintiff's side of the bar is to be proactive.

Targeted Tips: Labor Law

Representing management

The labor/employment overlap at management-side firms

Perhaps the most important thing to understand when seeking a job on the management side of the traditional labor practice is the overlap between the traditional labor and employment practices at most management-side firms. While some firms specialize in traditional labor relations, most management firms have a combined labor and employment department in which employment matters make up the lion's share of the work. If you are interested in traditional labor work you shouldn't expect to stroll into a position and work solely on labor matters. In fact, the opposite may be true, because you will likely start working on employment matters long before you are staffed on a traditional labor project.

A summer associate or junior attorney seeking traditional labor work should therefore be flexible and expect to work on a substantial number of employment matters in order to get involved in traditional labor relations work when it arises. Expressing an interest in employment law and taking classes that cover employment discrimination and other employment issues is always a good idea when trying to get your foot in the door at a management firm.

Keep abreast of labor trends

The same general rules for getting started on the management side in employment litigation apply in the traditional labor setting. Taking a labor law course that covers the NLRA is highly recommended, and any classes covering arbitration will also prove helpful. Staying informed on labor relations in general, who the major unions are and what kinds of tactics the modern labor movement uses is also a good way to demonstrate your interest in traditional labor law.

Getting a job on the union side

Take an assertive approach

Unions and union-side firms just don't recruit widely like the larger management-oriented firms, so you will have to be proactive to find a job representing labor. According to Ariana Levinson, a union-side lawyer and former AFL-CIO fellow, starting out on the union side definitely requires an assertive approach. These aren't the kind of jobs you will land at the standard on-campus interviewing. Direct mailings and networking with union attorneys are often the best way to find union-side opportunities. Labor-side firms tend to be much smaller than management firms and in-house positions at unions are even scarcer. In addition, attorneys with prior legal experience on the union side typically fill in-house positions, although in exceptional cases attorneys coming straight out of law school may find in-house union jobs.

Networking tips

To help overcome these recruiting obstacles and to locate union-side opportunities in your area you might want to start by contacting the AFL-CIO's Lawyers Coordinating Committee at (202) 637-5214), which will send interested law students their bulletin; you can also ask for a list of unions and union-side firms in your area. Joining the labor and employment section of your local bar as a student member will help you gain access to labor lawyers and labor law events. Remember that, as in any area of law, it is important to thoroughly research any employer you consider working for because there are a wide variety of approaches to practicing traditional labor law and you want to find one that fits your personality and philosophy. For example, when researching unions, you might look into the differences between public and private sector unions.

A "fire" for the labor movement

Candidates for union-side positions should clearly express their interest and commitment to union work. Nancy Hoffman, the general counsel of the Civil Service Employees Association (New York's largest public sector union), reports that nearly every attorney or intern who works in her legal department "possesses a certain 'fire' for the labor movement." This type of commitment is usually shown through prior work experience or extracurricular activity relating to the labor movement. Coursework that exposes you to federal labor laws is a good starting point, but more substantial activity is obviously preferred. Summer work at a union-side firm, an internship at a union or even volunteering for a union-sponsored activity like a political campaign all provide exposure to union-side activities and demonstrate an interest in union work. Prior union membership also shows a commitment to the labor movement and, along with any other relevant activity, should be specifically discussed in cover letters to potential employers.

Other Arenas

Working for the government

When considering a career in labor or employment law, don't forget about the public sector. Law firms, unions and large corporations aren't the only places to practice labor and employment law. The two federal agencies charged with enforcing federal employment and labor laws also maintain a substantial stable of attorneys. You might also look into employment opportunities at state agencies, like the Department of Fair Housing and Employment in California or the New York State Division of Human Rights.

The EEOC: a passion for civil rights

Those interested in enforcing employment laws might consider working for the EEOC. The hiring process at the EEOC begins at each individual office with the regional attorney in charge of the office. Although the regional attorneys' hands may be tied if agency officials in Washington haven't approved any vacancies, the EEOC always welcomes inquiries from qualified candidates. So don't let a temporary government hiring freeze (if one is in effect) deter you from contacting the agency. The steps you can take to make yourself a more attractive candidate to the EEOC are the same steps that make attorneys attractive to plaintiffs' side firms, because the EEOC is essentially looking for plaintiff-oriented lawyers. One caveat is that the EEOC generally hires lawyers with a few years of experience on the plaintiffs' side of the bar.

According to Katherine Bissell, the regional attorney in the EEOC's New York district office, the EEOC "looks for candidates who have demonstrated a passion for civil rights or employee rights to ensure that the candidate is committed to the EEOC's mission of eradicating discrimination in the workplace." One clear way to show an interest in working at the EEOC is do an internship at one of the regional offices. Almost every EEOC office has some sort of internship opportunity. Interested law students should contact each EEOC office directly; there is no need to go through the U.S. Office of Personnel Management. The EEOC's web site (www.eeoc.gov) provides extensive contact information and information on available job opportunities.

The NLRB: straddling the labor-management line

The NLRB has over 750 lawyers working for it in offices all across the country. About one-third of these attorneys work in the agency's main office in Washington, D.C. The NLRB is a great place to get started in traditional labor practice and offers valuable experience to new attorneys. In addition to the substantive work, the NLRB's role as referee between labor and management means that a position with the agency leaves open the doors on either side of the union-management divide should you decide to leave the NLRB for private practice.

As for getting hired at the NLRB, the same strategies for landing a management or union position apply. Showing interest in traditional labor and taking classes in this area is always one of the best things you can do. While the hiring process at the NLRB is erratic because of the ebbs and flows of the general budget, the NLRB is always interested in well-qualified law school graduates. The NLRB usually hires attorneys directly and, like the EEOC, does not need to go through the Office of Personnel Management. If you are interested in a position at the NLRB or would like to learn more about starting your career there, you should contact the NLRB directly. The NLRB has a comprehensive web site (www.nlrb.gov) with contact information, job opportunities and additional information on becoming an NLRB lawyer.

Going in-house

If serving a large corporation as an in-house employment lawyer sounds like your dream job, get in line. In-house positions are scarce, usually only available at the very largest companies and highly sought after by droves of experienced employment litigators. First and foremost, in-house employment lawyers need to be competent litigators who are familiar with the legal and factual issues that arise in labor and employment cases. The only way to get this kind of experience is to actually litigate cases. The path leading to an in-house position usually involves anywhere from three to over 10 years of experience as a management/defense litigator. Companies large enough to hire in-house employment lawyers don't want to pay for your training. They want to hire attorneys who have already been trained by the best employment firms around so that as an incoming lawyer you have immediate value as an experienced counselor.

First things first

In light of these experience requirements, the first step down the road to an in-house position is to forget about it. Forget about an in-house position and concentrate on becoming an excellent employment lawyer. Focus on starting out at a reputable management/defense firm where you will get valuable training from experienced attorneys. While some companies will only hire in-house lawyers that come from the most prestigious law firms, the only indispensable requirement for an in-house position is being a capable employment litigator and counselor. Starting at a firm where you will get substantive work early in your career is one of the best things you can do to ensure that you will become an excellent employment litigator.

Once you have the requisite experience for an in-house position it is hard to generalize about how you might find an opportunity. Legal recruiters are always an option, but many in-house attorneys find their positions through connections made while litigating at large management/defense firms. Some in-house lawyers are actually hired by former clients with whom they established close relationships.

Summary of Strategies

Take relevant law school courses

- Labor law and the NLRA
- Employment law, civil rights, Title VII and anti-discrimination laws
- Litigation and arbitration

Use your school's career services center

- Meet with career counselors
- Ask out about programs outside the large-firm recruitment process

Network

- Join labor & employment section of local bar associations
- Join specialized attorney organizations (e.g., NELA, ATLA)
- Contact national or local unions for nearby unions or union-side firms
- Talk to professors and practicing attorneys

Gain practical experience

- Moot court
- Clinics
- Internships
- Clerkships
- Union activities

Research firms

- Look into practice and clientele
- Ask about department model and nature of workload (e.g., Is it heavier on litigation or transactional matters? Do attorneys handle both employment and traditional labor work?)

Keep informed

- Trends of labor relations

- Major unions and modern labor movement tactics

- Employment discrimination and other workplace issues

Demonstrate your level of commitment

Especially important for plaintiffs' and union-side firms

Be proactive and do not get discouraged

APPENDIX

Job Search Resources

Glossary

Job Search Resources

The following list includes law firms, government agencies, unions and other organizations mentioned in this guide. The list is by no means a comprehensive index of all labor and employment career resources; for additional information, refer to the suggestions in Chapter Three on "Getting Hired," or contact your school's career services office.

Management and Defense-side Firms

Large national/international firms with labor and employment departments

*Akin, Gump, Strauss, Hauer & Feld, L.L.P.
Main office: Washington, D.C.
www.akingump.com

*Gibson, Dunn & Crutcher LLP
Main office: Los Angeles
www.gdclaw.com

*Jones, Day, Reavis & Pogue
Main office: Cleveland
www.jonesday.com

*McDermott, Will & Emery
Main office: Chicago
www.mwe.com

*Morgan, Lewis & Bockius LLP
Main offices: Philadelphia, New York, Washington, D.C.
www.morganlewis.com

*O'Melveny & Myers LLP
Main office: Los Angeles
www.omm.com

*Orrick, Herrington & Sutcliffe LLP
Main offices: New York, San Francisco
www.orrick.com

*Note: These firms were ranked among the top 10 firms in Labor & Employment by the 2003 Vault Guide to the Top 100 Law Firms.

*Paul, Hastings, Janofsky & Walker LLP
Main office: Los Angeles
www.paulhastings.com

*Proskauer Rose LLP
Main office: New York
www.proskauer.com

*Seyfarth Shaw
Main office: Chicago
www.seyfarth.com

*Skadden, Arps, Slate, Meagher & Flom LLP and Affiliates
Main office: New York
www.skadden.com

National or regional firms specializing in employment matters

Crosby, Heafey, Roach & May Professional Corporation
Main office: Oakland, Calif.
www.crosbyheafey.com

Fisher & Phillips LLP
Main office: Atlanta
www.laborlawyers.com

*Littler Mendelson, P.C.
Main office: San Francisco
www.littler.com

Employment boutiques

Benetar Bernstein Schair & Stein
Office: New York
www.benetar.com

Kauff McClain & McGuire LLP
Offices: New York, San Francisco
www.kmm.com

Swerdlow Florence Sanchez Swerdlow & Wimmer, a Law Corporation
Main office: Beverly Hills
www.swerdlowlaw.com

*Note: These firms were ranked among the top 10 firms in Labor & Employment by the 2003 Vault Guide to the Top 100 Law Firms.

Plaintiffs' Firms

Goldstein, Gellman, Melbostad, Gibson & Harris, LLP
Office: San Francisco
www.g3mh.com

Hadsell & Stormer, Inc.
Office: Los Angeles

Otis Canli & Duckworth LLP
Office: San Francisco
www.ocdlaw.com

Rudy, Exelrod & Zieff, L.L.P.
Office: San Francisco
www.reztlaw.com

Unions and Union-Side Firms

Union-Side Firms

Holguin & Garfield, APLC
Office: Los Angeles

Unions

AFL-CIO
www.aflcio.org/home.htm

AFL-CIO's Lawyers Coordinating Committee
Phone: (202) 637-5214

Civil Service Employees Association (New York's largest public sector union)
www.csealocal1000.net

Federal and State Agencies

U.S. Equal Employment Opportunity Commission (EEOC)
www.eeoc.gov

U.S. National Labor Relations Board (NLRB)
www.nlrb.gov

California Department of Fair Employment and Housing (DFEH)
ww.dfeh.ca.gov

New York State Division of Human Rights (DHR)
www.nysdhr.com

Bar Associations

Association of Trial Lawyers of America (ATLA)
www.atla.org
Phone: (800) 424-2727

California Employment Lawyers Association (CELA)
www.celaweb.org
Phone: (323) 653-6530

National Employment Lawyers Association (NELA)
www.nela.org
Phone: (415) 296-7629

NELA-New York
www.nelany.com
Phone: (212) 317-2291

Other NELA affiliates
www.nela.org/about/about_affiliates.htm

Glossary

Acronyms and Abbreviations

AAA: American Arbitration Association

ADA: Americans with Disabilities Act of 1990

ADEA : Age Discrimination in Employment Act of 1967

AFL-CIO: American Federation of Labor-Congress of Industrial Organizations

ALJ: administrative law judge

ATLA: Association of Trial Lawyers of America

CBA: collective bargaining agreement

CELA: California Employment Lawyers Association

DFEH: California Department of Fair Employment and Housing

DGA: Directors Guild of America

DHR: New York State's Division of Human Rights

EEOC: U.S. Equal Employment Opportunity Commission

ERISA: Employment Retirement Income Security Act of 1974

FEHA: California's Fair Employment and Housing Act

FEPA: state or local Fair Employment Practices Agency

FLSA: Fair Labor Standards Act of 1938

FMLA: Family and Medical Leave Act of 1993

LMRA: Labor Management Relations Act of 1947 (also known as the Taft-Hartley Act)

NELA: National Employment Lawyers Association

NLRA: National Labor Relations Act of 1935 (also known as the Wagner Act)

NLRB: U.S. National Labor Relations Board

PDA: Pregnancy Discrimination Act of 1978

SAG: Screen Actors Guild

Glossary

Appropriate bargaining unit: A group of employees with common job characteristics whom a union seeks to represent

Arbitration: A form of alternative dispute resolution commonly used to resolve labor-management disputes; the proceeding resembles but lacks the formality of civil litigation

Authorization cards: Cards stating that an employee wants a particular union to be its bargaining representative with the company; a union must obtain authorization cards from a certain percentage of employees in the appropriate bargaining unit in order to force an election

Collective bargaining agreement (CBA): Contract negotiated between union and employer to control the terms and conditions of employment

Concerted activities: Activities engaged in by employees/unions (like lawful picketing, boycotting and strikes) for the purpose of collective bargaining or other mutual aid or protection

Demand to Arbitrate: Serves the same purpose for arbitration as a complaint does for a civil trial; provides a brief statement of the dispute and the remedy sought

Disparate impact: A theory commonly used as the basis for class action discrimination suits under Title VII, in which the plaintiff class asserts that practices engaged in by the employer, whether intentionally discriminatory or not, disproportionately and adversely impact a protected class of employees

Disparate treatment: The basis for civil action under Title VII in which the plaintiff employee alleges that the employer intentionally discriminated against him or her based on a protected characteristic such as race, sex or age

Grievance process: The process for resolving grievances (disputes between employee and/or union and employer) outlined in the parties' collective bargaining agreement

Hostile work environment: A form of sexual harassment in which unwelcome sexual advances, requests for sexual favors or other conduct of a sexual nature are such that they unreasonably interfere with an employee's work performance or create an intimidating, hostile, or offensive working environment

Labor Management Relations Act of 1947 (also known as the Taft-Hartley Act or LMRA): An amendment to the National Labor Relations Act gives employees the right to refrain from participating in union activities and adds a series of prohibited unfair labor practices by unions

National Labor Relations Act of 1935 (also known as the Wagner Act or NLRA): The core federal statute of traditional labor relations law; intended to promote collective bargaining as a counterbalance to the inherent inequity in bargaining power between individual workers and management

Non-compete clause: A term of agreement between employee and employer under which employee agrees not to work for a competing company within a certain period of time after leaving the original employer

Protected characteristic: A trait or characteristic, such as race, color, sex, national origin or religion, protected under Title VII of the Civil Rights Act or equivalent state anti-discrimination law

"Quid pro quo" harassment: A form of sexual harassment in which a supervisor explicitly conditions a term of employment on the employee's submission to a request for sexual favors

Requests for information: Information requests exchanged between unions and employers, similar to discovery requests; disputes over how much information an employer or union is required to produce often result in unfair labor practice charges

Right to Sue Notice: A notice issued by the EEOC to a plaintiff who has filed a charge with the agency alleging that an employer discriminated against him or her; the notice, which is issued when the EEOC has decided not to take any action itself, permits the plaintiff to file suit in federal court

Secondary boycott: An unfair labor practice in which a union boycotts one employer to get that company to stop doing business with the company that the union really has a dispute with

Taft-Hartley Act: See "Labor Management Relations Act"

Title VII: Title VII of the 1964 Civil Rights Act, the foundation of the equal employment opportunity movement, prohibits an employer from discriminating against an employee or applicant with regard to hiring, firing, compensation, terms, conditions or privileges of employment based on protected characteristics including race, color, sex, national origin and religion

Trade secret: Confidential and proprietary information valuable to a company's business, such as a program, formula, device, method or technique

Unfair labor practices: activities prohibited by section 8 of the NLRA include practices which, if engaged in by employers or unions, result in a violation of employees' protected section 7 rights

Wagner Act: See "National Labor Relations Act"

About the Author

Timothy Grubb: Tim received his undergraduate degree in Communication from U.C. Santa Barbara and his Juris Doctorate (J.D.) from the UCLA School of Law. He is currently employed full time in the employment law department of a large management side law firm in California.

Vera Djordjevich: Vera is a writer and editor in New York. She holds a JD from New York University and a BA in history from Stanford University. A former litigator, she has worked as an editor at American Lawyer Media and is currently the senior editor of *On the Page* magazine (www.onthepage.org).

Psst...
Need a Change in Venue?

Use the Internet's most targeted job search tools for law professionals.

Vault Law Job Board

The most comprehensive and convenient job board for law professionals. Target your search by area of law, function, and experience level, and find the job openings that you want. No surfing required.

VaultMatch Resume Database

Vault takes match-making to the next level: post your resume and customize your search by area of law, experience and more. We'll match job listings with your interests and criteria and e-mail them directly to your inbox.

VAULT
> the most trusted name in career information™